PATIENT CARE AND PROFESSIONALISM

PATIENT CARE AND PROFESSIONALISM

Edited by

Catherine D. DeAngelis

OXFORD
UNIVERSITY PRESS

OXFORD
UNIVERSITY PRESS

Oxford University Press is a department of the University of Oxford.
It furthers the University's objective of excellence in research, scholarship,
and education by publishing worldwide.

Oxford   New York
Auckland   Cape Town   Dar es Salaam   Hong Kong   Karachi
Kuala Lumpur   Madrid   Melbourne   Mexico City   Nairobi
New Delhi   Shanghai   Taipei   Toronto

With offices in
Argentina   Austria   Brazil   Chile   Czech Republic   France   Greece
Guatemala   Hungary   Italy   Japan   Poland   Portugal   Singapore
South Korea   Switzerland   Thailand   Turkey   Ukraine   Vietnam

Oxford is a registered trademark of Oxford University Press
in the UK and certain other countries.

Published in the United States of America by
Oxford University Press
198 Madison Avenue, New York, NY 10016

© Oxford University Press 2014

Library of Congress Cataloging-in-Publication Data
Patient care and professionalism / edited by Catherine D. DeAngelis.
pages cm
Includes bibliographical references and index.
ISBN 978–0–19–992625–1—ISBN 978–0–19–992626–8   1. Medical personnel and
patient.   2. Physician and patient.   3. Physicians—Professional ethics.   4. Medical
laws and legislation.   I. DeAngelis, Catherine, 1940–
R727.3.P3634 2013
610.7306′9—dc23
2013004978

1 3 5 7 9 8 6 4 2
Printed in the United States of America
on acid-free paper

To patients everywhere and to the people who care for them.

CONTENTS

FOREWORD

Uwe E. Reinhardt, PhD

This much must be said first: The editor of this volume and the other distinguished authors who have contributed to it are to be congratulated and thanked for illuminating the role of professionalism in the care of patients in this unique way.

The medical literature on professionalism all too often presents only the introspective, and usually defensive, perspective of a profession under siege by the growing commercialism of modern medicine, by the often skeptical consumerism enabled by new information technology, and by a growing, general distrust of authority of any kind, including the authority traditionally reposing in the self-regulating professions such as medicine.

Refreshingly, this volume illuminates the topic from a variety of different perspectives, including those of physicians, patients, ethicists, legal experts, and practitioners in population health. Cast in this tradition of the liberal arts, the volume is the ideal platform for a course or a series of seminars that all schools for health professionals should offer their students.

But this must be said also: It is bold, if not reckless, for the editor and the authors to invite a blasphemous member of the dismal science to pen a Foreword to their work, one who years ago brashly engaged with the then-editor of *The New England Journal of Medicine,* Arnold S. Relman, in an infamous debate on the ethics of the medical profession—notably of organized medicine (Relman and Reinhardt, 1986). By now, both of us probably have mellowed some. Experience and more study certainly have given me a much more nuanced view on the matter.

Readers of this volume may be interested in the standard economic model of physician behavior that economists present to their students, including their pre-medical students. I recall describing it once in the pages of *The Journal of the American Medical Association* (*JAMA*), mainly to observe the predictably vehement reaction of physician-readers to that model (Reinhardt, 1999a).

In this model, physicians are cast in the role of the patient's conflicted agent, who at once helps patients formulate their demand for health-care goods and services but also derives an income (economists call it "profits") from rendering some or all of those services. In that model, professionalism appears as a variable representing a distaste for recommending and selling to patients particular physician services the physician knows to be medically unnecessary. But it is blithely assumed that physicians may do so nevertheless, either to achieve a target income or to compensate for declines in income brought about by reductions in fees or greater competition from colleagues. The elegant mathematical models in which these hypotheses are couched may be daunting to the mathematically challenged (Folland, Goodmand, and Stano, 2010; McGuire and Pauly, 1991); but, in a nutshell, this pretty much sums up the perspective of economics on medical professionalism in patient care.

An entertaining *Gedankenexperiment,* by the way, would be to turn this hard-nosed model of professional behavior on the economics "profession" itself; that is, to model the research findings produced by economists and their advice in the arena of public policy as the products of a trade-off between truth on one hand, as best as it can be inferred from a data set by a perfectly scrupulous economist, and, on the other, the added income or power that an economist could be earning by judiciously slanting these interpretations of the data to serve a paying client's interests or to serve the economist's own ideology about public policy.

To get a feel for the likely reactions of economists to such an insulting exercise, one need only behold the protestation of their innocence by the prominent economists who are featured in the documentary *Inside Job*, which chronicles events leading to the financial crisis of 2008–2009 and the role that these economists played in that development (*Inside Job*, 2010). These protestations notwithstanding, so stung by the documentary was the rest of the profession that it has now hastily and belatedly begun some timid steps toward articulating a code of ethics even for economists.

Lest readers write off economists too quickly as vaguely amusing exemplars of Oscar Wilde's definition of a cynic; namely, a person who "knows the price of everything and the value of nothing" (Wilde, 1892), let it be noted that members of the medical profession have given the world enough fodder to nourish a certain degree of skepticism about the role of classical "professionalism" in modern medicine. That skepticism, for example, is palpable in a series of papers on self-referral in imaging published in the December 2010 issue of *Health Affairs*, notably the rather jaundiced article by Bruce J. Hillman and Jeff Goldsmith, "Imaging: The Self-Referral Boom and the Ongoing Search for Effective Policies to Contain It" (Hillman and Goldsmith, 2010). There is also the claim in a recent report by the Institute of Medicine that in 2009 the U.S. health system wasted about $750 billion a year—about 30% of total national health spending—of which $210 billion represented unnecessary services and $75 billion, fraud (Colliver, 2012; Institute of Medicine, 2012).

In the modern vernacular, the word *professional* has become debased to the point that workers once known as "garbagemen" now prefer to be called "waste-disposal professionals." In sports, a "professional" player is one who is paid money for an activity often engaged in by amateurs. Elsewhere, "professionals" are thought to be people who possess certain well-defined technical skills, however they deploy them.

As the authors in this volume make clear, in the context of patient care, the word *professionalism* should stand for something much more than mere technical knowledge and skills. At its core, the professionalism sought for medicine is conceived of as a set of moral values that guide as well as constrain the physician's behavior in the conduct of medical practice and research. In discussing professionalism in dentistry, for example, Richard Masella views the attributes of a professional, beyond mere technical expertise and specialized knowledge, as "altruism, integrity, caring, community focus and a commitment to excellence" (Masella, 2007), a view echoed in much of the literature on professionalism in health care, the present volume included (Kirk, Lynne, 2007; Epstein and Hundert, 2002). The backbone of the "social trusteeship" implied by this conception is an obligation to put service to people before service to self (Masella, 2007).

With the trust that health-care professionals will actually adhere voluntarily to this implied social contract, without coercion through government regulation, society has delegated to the profession a good measure of authority in medicine. Its exercise is expected to be governed more by self-regulation by the moral principles implied by the word "professionalism" than by government edict. The late Eliot Freidson, one of the giants among sociologists writing on professionalism in general, and especially in medicine, saw in this ideal form of professionalism the "third logic" for a society; that is, the logical alternative to the logic of the free market and the logic of state bureaucracy (Freidson, 2001).

The question that has occupied much of the recent literature on professionalism in health care, once again including the authors of this volume, is the extent to which this ideal conception of professionalism has survived and can survive in a health system whose services are increasingly being commoditized, whose modus operandum is increasingly being commercialized, and in which patients increasingly are viewed, not only as objects of compassion, but as biological structures yielding cash flows that can be traded in the market (Reinhardt, 1999b).

It must be recognized that the untoward pressures on professionalism in medicine now discerned by its guardians are merely part of a wider trend to seduce professionals of any kind into the code of the free market. Part of that code is the belief that a person's income and wealth are faithful reflections of that person's contribution to society, a message still propagated in textbooks of economics, in spite of evidence to the contrary all around us. Another part of the market's code is the belief that professionalism alone cannot ever be relied upon to guide the conduct of professionals, but that good conduct requires appropriate government regulations, coupled with explicit financial incentives to elicit the desired professional behavior

First in the United States, but by now elsewhere in the world, for example, it is now taken for granted that good conduct by professional managers on behalf of the owners of business corporations can be elicited from the managers only through the provision of lavish financial incentives—cash bonuses, deferred compensation, stock grants, and stock options. The idea that genuine professional pride among corporate managers should be enough to beget the desired conduct is obsolete. Part of this bonus culture, albeit in forms tailored to nonprofit institutions, has by now crept even into academic health centers, although not so far into the rest of liberal arts academia.

In a culture that views a person's income and wealth as measures of their contribution to society and in which wealth is openly accorded worship, however insincere, not only by politicians (Johnson, 2009), but also by leaders of the nonprofit sector, it is perhaps not surprising that a decade or so after emerging from medical school and rigorous specialty training, many physicians look with dismay and possibly some envy at their former college classmates in business, law, and finance, where enormous wealth can so easily be earned in return for even quite modest contributions to society, or even highly negative contributions. There might come the temptation to view the moral code of professionalism in medicine as a shackle on the development of personal prosperity.

Given the debasement of professional standards elsewhere in the economy—not only in politics and in banking, but virtually everywhere—and given the open worship and the power of wealth in our society, it will take particular fortitude among health professionals to nourish and adhere to the professionalism on which society's trust in them still rests. My own impression, completely unscientific, is that, so far, the health professions have weathered the onslaught on their professionalism remarkably well—certainly better than has been the case among self-styled professionals elsewhere in the economy, with the exception of the military. We must thank the leaders of the medical profession, such as the authors of this volume, for leading the good fight on behalf of professionalism in the care of patients and medical research, and we must hope that they will prevail.

Professionalism in medicine alone, of course, cannot solve the problem of the immense waste in U.S. health care identified by the Institute of Medicine. Professionalism is too small a donkey to carry that load. But leaders of medicine could lead in efforts to remove some of the traditional obstacles to eliminating that waste, or at least make sure that the profession does not stand in the way of such efforts, as sometimes it has in the past.

References

Casselman B. Economists set rules on ethics. *Wall Street Journal,* January 9, 2012. Available at http://online.wsj.com/article/SB1000142405297020343690455 77148940410667970.html. Accessed December 6, 2012.

Colliver V. "Waste in U.S. health care system." *San Francisco Chronicle,* September 6, 2012.

Epstein RM, Hundert EM. Defining and assessing professional competence. *JAMA.* 2002;287(2): 226–235.

Folland S, Goodman AC, Stano M. Chapter 15. In: *The Economics of Health and Health Care.* 6th ed. 2010:299–308.

Freidson E. *Professionalism, the Third Logic: On the Practice of Knowledge.* 2001.

Hillman BJ, Goldsmith J. Imaging: The self-referral boom and the ongoing search for effective policies to contain it. *Health Aff.* 2010;29(12):2231–2236.

Inside Job, 2010: Video clip at http://www.imdb.com/title/tt1645089/. Accessed 12/6/12.

Institute of Medicine. *Best Care at Lower Cost: The Path to Continuously Learning Health Care in America.* 2012.

Johnson S. The quiet coup. *Atlantic Monthly,* May, 2009. Available at http://www. theatlantic.com/magazine/archive/2009/05/the-quiet-coup/307364/. Accessed December 7, 2012.

Kirk L. Professionalism in medicine: definitions and considerations for teaching. *Baylor U Med Proc.* 2007;20(1):13–16.

Masella, RS. Renewing professionalism in dental education: overcoming the market environment. *J Dent Educ.* 2007;71(2):205–216.

McGuire TG, Pauly MV. Physician response to fee changes with multiple payers. *J Health Econ.* 1991;10:385–410.

Reinhardt UE. The economist's model of physician behavior. *JAMA.* 1999a;281(5):462–465.

Reinhardt UE. Do you sincerely want to be rich? *Health Econ.* 1999b;8:355–362.

Relman AS, Reinhardt UE. Debating for-profit health care and the ethics of physicians. *Health Aff.* 1986;5:25–31.

Wilde O. Act III, *Lady Windermere's Fan.* 1892.

ACKNOWLEDGEMENTS

Special thanks to all authors who provided their expertise, time and resources and to all those who assisted them; to Veronica Green who took the "final" draft and provided the special skills of administrative assistants to produce the real final draft submitted to Oxford University Press (OUP), and to Joan Bossert, vice president and editorial director of OUP and her team including Miles Osgood and Prasad Tangudu, who rendered advice and encouragement.

CONTRIBUTORS

Professor Dame Carol Black, DBE, FRCP, FMedSci
Principal, Newnham College
Cambridge University

Clarence H. Braddock III, MD, MPH
Professor, Medicine
Associate Dean, Undergraduate and Graduate Medical Education
Director, Stanford Center for Medical Education, Research and Innovation
Stanford School of Medicine

Christine K. Cassel, MD
President and Chief Executive Officer, American Board of Internal Medicine and American Board of Internal Medicine Foundation

Adjunct Professor, University of Pennsylvania School of Medicine

Sir Cyril Chantler, MD, FRCP, FRCPCH
Chairman, University College London Partners
Academic Health Science Partnership
Professor, University College of London
Chair, UCL Partners

Sarah Davis, JD, MPA
Associate Director, Center for Patient Partnerships
Assistant Clinical Professor of Law
University of Wisconsin–Madison

**Catherine D. DeAngelis,
MD, MPH**
University Distinguished
  Service Professor, Emerita
Professor, Emerita, Johns
  Hopkins University
  Schools of Medicine
  (Pediatrics) and of Public
  Health (Health Policy and
  Management)
Editor in Chief, Emerita,
  JAMA, *Journal of the
  American Medical
  Association*

**Phil B. Fontanarosa,
MD, MBA**
Adjunct Professor, Emergency
  Medicine and Preventive
  Medicine
Northwestern University
  School of Medicine
Executive Editor, JAMA,
  *Journal of the American
  Medical Association*

**Patricia A. Fosarelli, MD,
D Min**
Associate Dean, The
  Ecumenical Institute of
  Theology
St. Mary's Seminary and
  University
Baltimore, Maryland

Martha E. Gaines, JD, LLM
Director, Center for Patient
  Partnerships
Associate Dean for Academic
  Affairs and Experiential
  Learning
Clinical Professor of Law
University of Wisconsin–
  Madison

**Lawrence O. Gostin, JD,
LLD (Hon)**
University Professor and
  Faculty Director
O'Neill Institute for National
  and Global Health Law
Georgetown University Law
  Center

Rachel Grob, MA, PhD
Director of National Initiatives
  and Scholar in Residence
Associate Clinical Professor,
  Center for Patient
  Partnerships
University of Wisconsin–
  Madison

James C. Harris, MD
Professor, Psychiatry and
  Behavioral Sciences,
  Pediatrics and Mental Health
Johns Hopkins University
  Schools of Medicine and of
  Public Health

James G. Hodge, JD, LLM
Lincoln Professor of Law
    and Ethics
Sandra Day O'Connor College
    of Law
Arizona State University

Eric S. Holmboe, MD, PhD
Senior Vice President and Chief
    Medical Officer
American Board of
    Internal Medicine
    Foundation

Howard Markel, MD, PhD
George E. Wantz Distinguished
    Professor of the History of
    Medicine
Professor of Pediatrics and
    Communicable Diseases
Director, Center for the History
    of Medicine
The University of Michigan
    Medical School

Uwe E. Reinhardt, PhD
James Madison Professor
    of Political Economy and
    Professor of Economics and
    Public Affairs
Princeton University

Mark J. Schlesinger, PhD
Professor, School of
    Public Health
Yale University

**Kathleen M. White, PhD,
    RN, NEA-BC, FAAN**
Associate Professor,
    Department of Acute and
    Chronic Care
Johns Hopkins University
    School of Nursing

INTRODUCTION

The odyssey, that for me was truly an intellectual quest, resulting in this text began a number of years ago when I was asked by a colleague, Joan Bossert of Oxford University Press, to write a book on medical professionalism. I agreed to do so, with two provisos: I would not begin that project until I had stepped down from the editorship of the *Journal of the American Medical Association*, and the book would be written from the perspectives of the health care team centered on the patient. She agreed, and this book became an embryonic thought, or rather numerous thoughts.

The first step in organizing this book was to find authors with expertise in professionalism and with excellent writing skills. Fortunately, I had little trouble identifying those individuals, and no one turned down my request for them to become a partner in this initiative. I never cease to be amazed that the best authors are those who are extremely busy but find time to write. They do this knowing that the financial return for such labor approximates the cost of lunch at a fast-food restaurant. Clearly this and similar works are labors of love, and I am very grateful that my author colleagues for this book are such individuals.

Except for textbooks, I generally dislike edited books because they are organized like a group of individual silos and read with little or no central theme. However, having passed through the "puberty rituals" of nursing, medicine, and public health, and having had far too many experiences as a patient myself, I was convinced that the very nature of this book required the expertise of many, and no single author could possibly cover all professions involved in the health care of patients. To mitigate the choppy nature of edited texts, and with the approval of the authors, I have edited every chapter, attempting to maintain the single theme and the flow, while maintaining the individual expertise and personality of the authors. What else would a former editor-in-chief of a major journal do? If I have failed to accomplish this, please accept my apologies; I have tried my best.

ORDER OF CHAPTERS

The *Foreword* sets the stage for the general theme of the book, with sometimes tongue-in-cheek style to make major points. The chapters are ordered so that the main "character" in this book, the patient, has the first voice, followed by the ancient history of professionalism, the recent resurrection of professionalism in the United Kingdom (U.K.), followed by professionalism in the United States (U.S.). The next chapters cover the various health care professions: medicine, nursing, public health, law, leadership, religion, and finally a chapter on the science (yes, the science!) of professionalism. Every chapter is written by internationally known experts.

BASIC CONTENT OF EACH CHAPTER

Because my goal herein is to introduce the reader to each chapter, I often quote from what the author wrote in the chapter. Because

I don't want to overwhelm the pages with quotation marks, I have not cloaked all direct quotes in such marks.

Chapter 1, whose lead author is a long-term survivor of ovarian cancer and has extensive experience in clinician–patient relationships, examines the intersection of professionalism and patient advocacy. Specifically, the authors explore concepts such as what makes a "medical home" a home; the physician's responsibility not merely to deliver health care, but to ensure its receipt; the treasure trove that is team-based care; and the tender trap of guidelines, evidence- based medicine, and measurement. The chapter concludes with the authors reflecting on emerging models in professional education and practice that value the grace of "leading from behind" and the ultimate healing power of humility.

Chapter 2 approaches professionalism using the original words and ultimate meaning of the Hippocratic Oath, which was probably the first oath taken by a health care professional. Using the Hippocratic Oath as a case study, the author discusses the philosophy of many texts, collectively classified as Hippocratic, taken by medical students upon graduation. The symbolic act of oath-taking serves as a powerful reminder and declaration that physicians are all part of something much larger, older, and more important than a specific era, specialty, or institution. Given the current social quandaries facing almost every aspect of medicine, the need for physicians to make a formal warrant of diligent, moral, and ethical conduct and values in the service of patients may be stronger than ever.

Chapter 3 deals with professionalism and politics in the United Kingdom. Since politics is an intricate component of professionalism in every country, it is appropriate for a country (kingdom) with such a long history to be the site of the resurrection of professionalism in modern history. Even though the single-payer system is not how health care is paid for in the United States and some other developed countries, the approach to professionalism in the U.K. has many components pertinent to the U.S. and other countries.

The authors discuss what was and is being done to bolster professionalism in the face of more effective, complex, but also dangerous medical care. Currently, the trust and confidence patients place in their physicians are tempered by explicit standards of knowledge, skills, experience, attitudes, conduct, and value judgments necessary for continuing practice; all of these are components of regulation. The values of medical professionalism and of society, the aims of government to improve quality and safety, and the clinical and cost-effectiveness of care are not dissimilar and should reinforce each other.

Chapter 4 deals with the role of specialty boards in promoting professionalism, using the American Board of Internal Medicine (ABIM) as the case study. This is appropriate, since the ABIM and the ABIM Foundation were born from the efforts of the medical profession to establish credible standards for physician specialists to serve the public. The authors discuss the important role of specialty boards in promoting professionalism and how this role has expanded to include advocacy, scholarship, and collaboration.

Chapter 5 explores modern professionalism, including the various characteristics and attributes (primarily) of a physician. The physician's interactions with patients; medical, nursing, legal, business, religious, and other colleagues; and students in the clinical, educational, research, and administrative environments are approached from the individual to societal responsibilities.

Chapter 6 covers professionalism and nursing. Because it is the sole chapter specifically on nursing, it is one of the longest in the book. The author discusses the history of nursing professionalism from Florence Nightingale to the twenty-first century; the development of nursing as a profession, defining how nursing meets the concept of professionalism and what professionalism in nursing currently means. Nurses' commitment to caring, competence, life-long learning, and strong ethical values; the pursuit of autonomy, accountability, and responsibility for practice; the demonstration of collaboration and collegiality; and the application of knowledge are discussed. Finally, the author addresses the question of whether professionalism in nursing is still a quest or fully accomplished and should no longer exist.

Chapter 7 explores professionalism, considering the public or a population as the "patient." The author explores the vital impor-tance of the health, safety, and well-being of the population and argues that safeguarding the public's health requires collaboration and partnership between public health and clinical professionals. The author discusses important synergies between public health and clinical practice and defines public health law and how that law can advance public health.

Chapter 8 explores the role of law and legal systems in the thera-peutic relationship between clinicians and patients. The author discusses legal professionalism among practitioners, including licensure of clinicians and health care institutions, scope of prac-tice, standards of care, and liability. The evolving legal structure underlying health care delivery and professionalism, protecting patients, and end-of-life decisions are discussed in depth. After reading this chapter, I believe the reader will agree with the author, who concludes that the role of law within the therapeutic relation-ship is profound, controversial, and politically charged.

Chapter 9 covers professionalism and fiduciary responsibilities in health care leadership. The author discusses fiduciary relation-ships and responsibilities involved therein, leadership and profes-sionalism in health care organizations, and professional standards and competencies for health care leaders. The author stresses that professionalism goes beyond clinical areas, extending into the role of the health care professional as a leader who must embody the highest principles of professionalism.

Chapter 10 covers the role of religion in professionalism. The author addresses the definition and goals of religion and discusses how the major religions (Buddhism, Christianity, Hinduism, Islam, Judaism, and Sikhism) understand the importance of the care of others, which must be considered in the clinical settings. The author further discusses what major religions say about medical care.

Chapter 11 covers the science behind professionalism, or as the author states, the science of care is a basis for the art of medicine. The author discusses the psychobiological framework for patient- centered care, psychology and physiology of social engagement, trust as meaningful social engagement, caution and anxiety (i.e., increased autonomic arousal and vigilance), demoralization, despair, the downward spiral from trust to demoralization and despair, attachment style, eliciting the patient's narrative, the placebo response, patient-centered treatment, and realistic hope. An included case report from Engel's Vestermark Award lecture illustrates much of what is discussed in this chapter.

FINAL COMMENT

The goal of this book is to provide the reader with a concise, easy-to-read text that summarizes the complexities involved in patient care and professionalism. If this fails to so inform the reader, the fault is all mine in misjudging the needs of all involved in patient care. If so, mea culpa. If we have succeeded, the authors and I will bask in the joy of knowing we have made small steps toward helping our professions grow.

Chapter 1

Medical Professionalism from the Patient's Perspective

Is There an Advocate in the House?

MARTHA E. GAINES, RACHEL GROB,
MARK J. SCHLESINGER, AND SARAH DAVIS

INTRODUCTION

The medical profession, like other guilds, was left to define its own notions of professionalism relatively unfettered, from the earliest days until the modern era. But from the time when "patients" were patient, until now, much has changed for physicians and the patients they see. Professionalism in medicine, once delineated by twin notions of "autonomy" and "altruism," is now being reexamined to see if more collaborative values such as "interdependence," "team-based care" and "advocacy" might find a home there.

Team-based care and the interdependence implicated in the concept have enjoyed growing attention in professional medical literature (Davis et al., 2005; Mitchell et al., 2012). Although initially driven by efforts to improve the quality and efficiency of medical care, medical educators, ethicists, and professional associations have more recently begun to explore the implications these hold for professional norms. While still in its preliminary stages, this shift in professional expectations has been quite pervasive, albeit partly obscured by the use of different descriptors for different specialties—"patient-centered care" and "medical homes" for primary care physicians, "teamwork" for hospital-based clinicians (Bleakley, 2006; Braddock et al., 2004; Mitchell et al., 2012).

Likewise, vigorous discussions about the proper role of "advocacy" if any, for physicians have come to feature prominently in medical literature over the past several years (Flynn, 1995; Gruen et al., 2004, 2006; Earnest et al., 2010). Organizations at the crux of medical professionalism—including the ACGME, the ABIM Foundation, and the AMA—all describe advocacy as integral to practice in the twenty-first century (Nasca et al., 2012; ABIM 2002; AMA 2001). Nonetheless, expectations about the nature and extent of this role remain poorly defined and deeply contested; the battle lines range from challenges to the notion of physicians as advocates at all, to appropriate levels or domains of advocacy, to how to distinguish required from voluntary advocacy. And those responsible for medical education wonder anxiously about how to teach students, and evaluate their competency, in an as-yet-undefined skill set (Rothman, 2000; Stern and Papadakis, 2006; Palfrey, 2006; Dharamsi et al., 2011).

We are encouraged by this attention in medical professionalism to increasing collaboration between patients, health care professionals, and others key to the care equation. It is a refreshing approach to the epidemic of fractured, uncoordinated care—particularly where patients are enfranchised as full members of the team. As educators, we see aspiring young individuals begin medical education with a strong, natural inclination to advocate with their patients for appropriate care. We hope this chapter will support them as they strive to redesign practice systems so that professionals can join with colleagues and patients to advocate for better health and health care.

Each of this chapter's authors is a patient, an advocate, and an educator. Collectively we have more than sixty years of experience doing direct service, as well as community, policy, and legislative health advocacy. Likewise, we have decades of experience teaching future physicians and other professionals together, inside and outside the classroom. We also draw heavily here from more than a decade of experience at the Center for Patient Partnerships at the University of Wisconsin–Madison, educating professional students across the disciplines of medicine, nursing, pharmacy, and law to advocate directly with thousands of patients who have sought our help as they struggled to get the care they needed (Hurst et al., 2008).

We hope our collective experience allows us to shine some light on professionalism from a different angle, revealing the way to a new kind of relationship for patients and physicians of the future—a rebirth of trust born in real collaboration. We also endeavor here to introduce the patient's voice into this rich conversation. We begin with a discussion of what we mean by the term "advocacy" in the practice of medicine, and then offer perspectives on where opportunities for medical advocacy lie, the rich collaborations they engender, and ways to overcome systemic barriers to advocacy.

ADVOCACY DEFINED

An "advocate" is defined as a person who speaks on behalf of others, on behalf of a cause or argument, and, more recently, who helps others speak up for themselves. It derives from the Old French *avocat* (lawyer) and before that from the Latin *advocare*—to call for or speak on behalf of (Wiktionary, 2012; Merriam-Webster, 2012). Although "advocacy" was originally a descriptor for the work of courtroom lawyers, helping others find their voices, and speaking on their behalf until then, can be seen as an essential arrow in the quiver of many helping professions.

Our conception of advocacy includes two key elements: a set of functional roles, and an animating spirit. The roles (Table 1.1)

Table 1.1 ADVOCACY ROLES AT THE HEART OF PROFESSIONALISM

Advocacy Role	Specific Aspects of Each Role
Empathic Listener	Hears what people are unable to articulate in words
	Lets others know they've been heard
Effective Communicator	Finds a way to connect empathically with others
	Offers information that mobilizes effective action
Counselor	Helps others clarify their values and aspirations
	Encourages others to envision and embrace change
Diagnostician	Understands complexity of contexts and problems
	Explains complicated causality in understandable ways
Conductor (orchestral)	Builds bridges and promotes collaboration
	Unites diverse communities into effective coalitions
Caring Carefully Across Cultures	Has a nuanced feel for the complexity of culture
	Connects across cultural/social domains

Table 1.1 (Continued)

Advocacy Role	Specific Aspects of Each Role
Catalyst for Change	Challenges problematic practices and inspires useful ones
	Undaunted by inertia and allegiance to the status quo
Lifelong Learner	Practices critical self-reflection and models self-care
	Committed to transparency and disclosure
Capacity Builder	Appreciates, inspires, and nurtures leadership in others
	Supports empowerment and self-advocacy
Boundary Spanner/ Interpreter	Applies lessons from other times, places, and domains
	Cultivates interdependence and integrates individual and systems perspectives
Transformational Leader	Envisions and articulates how change is possible, even in hard circumstances
	Constructively alters fundamental presumptions about health and health care

describe a broad range of skills and capacities crucial for effective advocacy. Skills, however, are not enough. Advocacy is dauntingly hard work, especially in the context of the American health care system. The hard work of advocating for others can only be sustained at the nexus where, to paraphrase Frederick Buechner, the things that give you joy intersect with the needs of the world (Buechner, 1973). Advocacy opportunities in any given situation can thus be seen as a moveable feast—depending as they do on how the particular need interacts with one's gifts, skills, interests, and training. Through this lens, advocacy in the realm of medical professionalism is more a function of who the physician is, the nature and context of his or her practice, and what his or her particular patients need—and less a standardized or prescribed set of actions.

The medical profession has a rich tradition of advocacy in practice and scholarship, and practicing physicians advocate every day on behalf of their patients. When listening deeply, discerning illness and its cause, exploring patient values, researching and explaining treatment options, untangling insurance coverage barriers, and identifying ways for uninsured patients to access care, physicians are advocating in the purest sense of the word.

While advocacy is often an integral part of clinical practice, the question remains what kind of advocacy can reasonably be expected of physicians in the course of their practices. Debate in the major medical journals has focused both on the relative wisdom of physician advocacy and the type of advocacy that can be deemed core to medical professionalism (Gruen et al., 2004, 2006; Earnest et al., 2010). Most physicians understand only too well how vital it is for their patients to have advocates both in and outside the clinical encounter. But even those most inclined to serve as effective advocates for their patients wonder what physician advocacy properly entails, how they can learn the necessary skills, and where to find the requisite time for it.

These questions are further complicated because the "needs of the world" are changing in some profound ways, creating both new obligations for medical professionals and new opportunities for meeting professional norms in the context of a broader multi-professional team. On one hand, insurance arrangements from both public and private payers are shifting, with an increased emphasis on so-called consumer-directed health plans (Robinson and Ginsburg, 2009). These high-deductible policies force patients into an ever more expansive role as informed consumers, expected to assess the value, not simply of a given medical procedure, but of an entire course of clinical treatment. In most cases, this would be implausible without close collaboration, assistance, and advice by their clinicians, which is made more challenging because insurance companies continue to render their terms and practices in language so obscure that future coverage is difficult to anticipate and hardly assured (Schoen et al., 2010).

Fortunately, physicians can increasingly turn to other professionals to assist with these aspects of advocacy. In recent years, there has been a dramatic growth in the availability of patient navigators, community health workers, and patient advocates, all oriented to addressing the challenges of long-term coordination of benefits, clarifying uncertainties about coverage, and dealing with issues regarding access (Manderson et al., 2012). The health care reforms under the auspices of the Patient Protection and Affordable Care Act of 2010 provided new government funding and direction to these forms of consumer assistance (Grob et al., 2013). This means physicians can partner increasingly often with others to assure that needed advocacy is available to the patient even if the physician is not capable of or suited to advocacy in a given situation. Where physicians do not yet have such relationships, they often play a strategic role in identifying and building a stronger advocacy infrastructure in their communities.

ADVOCACY OPPORTUNITIES

Opportunities for advocacy vary physician by physician, depending on where the things that bring them joy intersect with the needs of the world. Professionally and personally, most of us find the things that bring us joy are a function of fundamental attributes about us: who we are, how effective we can be, what training we have acquired or can seek, and what piques our interest. The needs of the world are perhaps more apparent, but need not be limited to the broad societal contexts of hunger, poverty, housing, or health care access. Finding joy in nurturing caring connections with individual patients is by any definition advocacy—it is joy meeting need in the quintessential, medical sense.

In the course of our teaching and advocacy work we have described eleven distinct roles advocates play in a health care context (Table 1.1). Although some are more commonly associated with traditional practice in the exam room, all are valuable both in and outside the clinic setting, and on behalf of individual patients as well as their communities. We have selected a half dozen for illustration here—communicator, diagnostician, boundary spanner, catalyst for change, conductor, and capacity-builder—all of which are practiced every day by physicians in a wide variety of settings and contexts. The case example we use here is real, though identifying characteristics and a number of details have been altered.

Jane's Dilemma

Dr. G called the Center for Patient Partnerships (CPP) for help with a new patient of his, Jane, who recently told him she had thousands of dollars of denied insurance claims. She had had elective bariatric weight loss surgery five years ago, which she paid for out of pocket. She fully understood all along that her insurance company would not pay for any medical services related to the surgery. However, since the operation, whenever Jane visited any doctor for any reason, her claim was denied. When Jane inquired, the insurance company told her it was because the services were related to her bariatric surgery, which they were not.

Despite repeated payment denials, Jane had not spoken with any of her prior physicians about the problem, until she met Dr. G, her new primary care physician, who seemed warm, kind, and attentive. Even as she told Dr. G about the problem, he noticed she seemed timid; she said she would understand if it weren't the type of thing he could help her address. It didn't take him long to see that she was embarrassed about her obesity, about the surgery, and about her marginal weight gain in the ensuing five years. She told him she knew she was responsible for any care related to the surgery, but didn't feel it was fair that all subsequent care was not covered. Dr. G listened carefully, and assured her that he considered her present care to be unrelated to her earlier surgery and that his clinic billing office would see that the matter was resolved.

Dr. G soon learned that the billing office was very familiar with Jane's insurance woes as they had been dealing with the issue for the past several years, since Jane first came to the clinic. Despite their having explained that the surgery was several years in the past and that her present care was not related to it, the clinic was still required to list her history of surgery as one of her diagnoses on claims sent to the insurance company. A claim usually has many different diagnoses listed; some of Jane's had twenty or more.

The billing office was told Jane's claims were routinely denied because the insurer had, as a "safety precaution," set their system to automatically place bariatric surgery at the top of the diagnosis list, regardless of where it appeared on the patient's claim history. Then, with bariatric surgery as the primary diagnosis, the claim would be automatically denied. Despite numerous attempts, they were not able to get the insurance company to change its practices. When the insurance representative was asked whether it was the company's intention not to pay for any of Jane's care, she assured them it was not. When asked how the automatic relisting and denials could be abated, she said she did not know.

Frustrated by what he heard, Dr. G recommended his finance office supervisor call the Center for Patient Partnerships (CPP) and explain Jane's situation and the office's concern that other patients might also be affected by this practice. The CPP assigned a student advocate who researched the issues and, after consulting with his faculty supervisor, filed a complaint with the Office of the Commissioner of Insurance explaining the problem and arguing the insurer was denying claims in bad faith. Within days, the insurance company called Dr. G's office to notify them that they were changing their policy with regard to bariatric surgery; their system would no longer automatically deny claims that have bariatric surgery listed among the diagnoses. Instead, a claim would only be denied if bariatric surgery is one of the first four diagnoses listed. They further indicated they would pay all of Jane's back claims, including several she had already paid herself, fearing the impact of unpaid bills.

Dr. G, delighted with this resolution, called the CPP to thank them, and to suggest they follow up with area health care institutions to ensure this issue is resolved not just for Jane, but for all bariatric patients. For her part, Jane, newly encouraged by this outcome, set about to resolve similar outstanding billing issues with several other clinics.

ADVOCACY REFLECTIONS

It was his skill as a communicator that was central to Dr. G's resolution of Jane's billing problem and, potentially, to the effective continuation of her care. Although the problem had existed for several years, Dr. G was the first physician to put Jane at ease enough to talk about it. After their brief conversation, Dr. G raised the issue with his billing supervisor and listened to her tale of repeated unsuccessful attempts to resolve the matter satisfactorily.

Dr. G, as diagnostician, looked beyond clinical assessment and perceived that Jane had been struggling alone with this billing issue for several years. He also sensed that her struggle with obesity may have increased both her vulnerability to insurance denials and the likelihood that she would suffer these alone. Hearing the depth of Jane's frustration, and inclined to think this was not a matter she could effectively resolve alone, Dr. G offered to have his office tackle the troubling billing issues.

In his role as boundary spanner, Dr. G ultimately concluded that resolution of the issue required a set of skills not present in his office. Among the community resources he regularly consulted, the CPP was an organization with experience researching and resolving complex insurance issues, so he had his office call to secure an independent advocate for Jane.

Dr. G, as catalyst for change, explained his concern that individuals who have struggled with obesity might be particularly likely not to seek help with insurance denials because shame related to the condition exacerbates the confusion they—like all patients— often feel in the face of complex insurance plans that are difficult for even highly educated consumers to understand. The CPP advocate shared Dr. G's concern and followed up with the Commissioner of Insurance and area hospitals and clinics to ensure these denials were remedied, not just for Jane, but for all similarly situated patients. As Dr. G reflected further on Jane's experience, he realized it was a good time to revisit with his entire staff the importance of proactivity and problem solving when system-level problems arise. He also established short, monthly staff meetings to ensure that, going forward, staff would have a forum where they can raise these issues.

The breadth of Dr. G's collaborations in Jane's interest was considerable, but the time he spent personally was not. In the limited time he had available, he served a strategic conductor role, engaging his billing supervisor, outside advocates, and (indirectly) the Commissioner of Insurance's office to help resolve this issue for his patient and address it for others similarly affected. Effective physician advocates, like all advocates, know that, while they can often take direct action themselves, they must also call on others to be efficacious. Professional office staff, community workers, social workers, lawyers, free-standing patient advocates, and others can be critical partners for physicians, and are often positioned to be powerfully effective (Lown and Kalet, 2008).

Finally, Dr. G. acted as a capacity-builder, teaming up with Jane to address the barrier to health and health care she was encountering. After absorbing Jane's words and feelings, Dr. G determined she needed a jump-start to address the denials since she did not yet have requisite knowledge or assurance. However, once the first denials were reversed, Dr. G. observed Jane's renewed confidence in her own ability to advocate for resolution of other medical bills and understood it was time to pull back from a direct role in the process.

Although historically overlooked, underestimated, or deemed not responsible for advocacy on their own behalf, patients have the greatest inherent stake in both processes and outcomes related to their care. However, many patients have been so thoroughly disempowered by our daunting health care financing and delivery system that they have lost all hope of influencing their own health care and outcomes. Attentive, meaningful advocacy reengages patients, enabling them to once again "...counteract the deadening effect of other people always making decisions on [their] behalf...." (Jufessur et al., 2009). While responsibility for individual self-advocacy and health care system improvement certainly cannot rest on patients' shoulders alone, patients are a powerful, often untapped source for advocacy in both domains (Hoffman et al., 2011).

ADVOCACY AHEAD

It has been said that if the twentieth century was about "thinking the world apart," then the twenty-first century must be about "thinking it back together again." Progress in preventing, diagnosing, and treating disease over the last century was extraordinary; many modern-day physicians remark how dramatically the practice of medicine has changed, even in the course of their lifetimes. Success in managing disease is, in part, a result of focusing intensively on the physiology of disease as distinct from the patient who has it. But this separation comes at a cost. Physicians and patients would benefit from a renewed focus on the humanity that connects us all, and informs the life-and-death decisions we face together every day. As Sir William Osler reminded us more than a century ago, "It is much more important to know what sort of a patient has a disease than what sort of a disease a patient has" (Osler, 1904).

Tomorrow's physicians will need solid relationships with their patients as they navigate together the increasingly complex, costly options for medical intervention and ensure patients make real choices based on their particular values for the balance between quality and quantity of life. They will also have to be robustly educated as strong, skilled advocates. Recent movement toward interdisciplinary medical education is promising, though still in early stages of development. To date, most physician advocates have been self-taught, learning by doing in response to their patients' needs.

The search for an advocacy curriculum for medical students and practicing physicians has begun, and fortunately it need not be created from whole cloth (Earnest et al., 2010; Dharamsi et al., 2011). There are existing models, including several where interdisciplinary collaboration and education flourish already—the National Center for Medical-Legal Partnership, Health Leads, and the Center for Patient Partnerships (National Center for Medical-Legal Partnerships,

2012; Health Leads, 2012; Center for Patient Partnerships, 2012). Successful programs are grounded in intentional learning communities where all involved—teachers, students, and patients—are known simply as learners. They also engender: critical self-reflection; interdisciplinary cross-pollination; collaborative, non-hierarchical teamwork; and experiential learning that involves faculty, students, and patients joining together to advocate for needed care on a case-by-case basis or at the system level (Conrad et al., 2012; Fink, 2003; Haworth & Conrad, 1997). Including patients as collaborators in the education of young physicians is vital if they are to learn how to team up with their patients. Over more than a decade at the Center for Patient Partnerships, we have observed that medical students who have the opportunity to learn in this type of setting are more likely to listen carefully to their patients; to approach practice with a well-formed understanding of their patients' goals, values, and priorities; and to support active engagement by patients in their own care. They know how to identify and address the multifactorial problems that arise in their patients' lives and to appreciate the roles other professionals can play. They develop a habit of collaboration in the course of their practices, and are better equipped to determine when to refer these patients to other professionals. These physicians also have a network of former classmates they can tap as skilled allies in advocacy.

Above all, prospective clinicians educated in this way know they must have an advocacy plan: a way to ensure their patients get the right care in the right place at the right time. They learn every day, as they practice advocacy alongside colleagues from a wide variety of disciplines, that while they need not personally execute every advocacy function, physicians must ensure that care is effectively received by their patients, and not merely "delivered."

Beneath much of the discourse about the proper role of advocacy in medical professionalism is a significant pragmatic concern about financial incentives. Simply put, it is unrealistic to imagine that physicians will spend the time required to tackle the non-clinical barriers to care—listening as patients describe them, engaging other professionals to help resolve them, or reforming the systems that spawn them—without adequate compensation. But there is hope that physicians, who are deeply committed to their patients' health in the fullest sense, will see that commitment recognized in concrete outcomes evaluation and compensation formulations. Recent progress toward health reform includes initiatives to align physician compensation more directly with what patients need and want. Still, many of these reforms are incorporated into the PPACA as demonstration projects, or as administrative changes that will take years to refine and translate into practice (Grob et al., 2013; Skocpol, 2010). To ensure that these promises become reality, strong system-level advocacy by all concerned with the future of health care will be necessary.

ADVOCACY PROMISE

In his writing about professionalism, Parker Palmer raises this soulful question for all professionals: "How do I stay close to the passions and commitments that took me into this work—challenging myself, my colleagues, and my institution to keep faith with this profession's deepest values?" (Palmer, 2007). Each medical student's spirited desire to help others is a sacred trust—one we cannot afford to squander. If future physicians are to fulfill their professional promise to care carefully for their patients, we must equip them as effective advocates with a sustainable plan for ensuring that their patients surmount barriers to needed care, and that their own professional energy is spent in that place where the things that give them joy intersect with the needs of the world.

References

ABIM Foundation, American Board of Internal Medicine; ACP-ASIM Foundation, American College of Physicians–American Society of Internal Medicine; European Federation of Internal Medicine. Medical professionalism in the new millennium: a physician charter. *Ann Intern Med.* 2002;136:243–246.

American Medical Association. Declaration of Professional Responsibility: Medicine's social contract with humanity. Available at http://www.ama-assn.org/ama/upload/mm/369/decofprofessional.pdf. Published December 4, 2001. Accessed October 12, 2012.

Bleakley A. A common body of care: the ethics and politics of teamwork in the operating theater are inseparable. *J Med Philos.* 2006;31:305–322.

Braddock CH III, Eckstrom E, Haidet P. The "new revolution" in medical education: fostering professionalism and patient-centered communication in the contemporary environment. *J General Intern Med.* 2004;19(5 Pt 2):610–611. doi: 10.1111/j.1525–1497.2004.45003.x

Buechner F. *Wishful Thinking: A Theological ABC.* New York: Harper & Row; 1973.

Center for Patient Partnerships. Available at www.patientpartnerships.org. Accessed October 19, 2012.

Conrad C, Dunek L. *Cultivating Inquiry-Driven Learners: A College Education for the 21st Century.* Baltimore, MD: Johns Hopkins University Press; 2012.

Davis K, Schoenbaum SC, Audet AM. A 2020 vision of patient-centered primary care. *J Gen Intern Med.* 2005;20:953–957. doi: 10.1111/j.1525–1497.2005.0178.x

Dharamsi S, Ho A, Spadafora SM, Wollard R. The physician as health advocate: translating the quest for social responsibility into medical education and practice. *Acad Med.* 2011;86:1108–1113.

Earnest MA, Wong SL, Federico SG. Perspective: Physician advocacy: what is it and how do we do it? *Acad Med.* V 2010;85:63–67.

Fink, LD. *Creating Significant Learning Experiences: An Integrated Approach to Designing College Courses.* San Francisco: Jossey-Bass; 2003.

Flynn MB. Power, professionalism, and patient advocacy. *Am J Surg.* 1995;170:407–409.

Grob RM, Schlesinger S, Davis D, Cohen J, Lapps A. Capstone for patient empowerment: consumer assistance programs under the PPACA. *Health Aff (Millwood).* 2013: forthcoming

Gruen RL, Pearson SD, Brennan TA. Physician-citizens—public roles and professional obligations. *JAMA.* 2004;291:94–98.

Gruen RL, Campbell EG, Blumenthal D. Public roles of US physicians: community participation, political involvement, and collective advocacy. *JAMA.* 2006;296:2467–2475.

Haworth JG, Conrad C. *Emblems of Quality in Higher Education: Developing and Sustaining High-Quality Programs.* Boston: Allyn and Bacon; 1997.

Health Leads. www.healthleadsusa.org Accessed October 19, 2012.

Hoffman B, Tomes N, Grob R, Schlesinger M. *Patients as Policy Actors.* New Brunswick, NJ: Rutgers University Press; 2011.

Hurst M, Gaines M, Grob R, Weil L, Davis S. Educating for health advocacy in settings of higher education. In: Earp J, French E, Gilkey M, eds. *Patient Advocacy for Health Care Quality: Strategies for Achieving Patient-Centered Care.* Boston: Jones and Bartlett Publishers; 2008.

Jufessur T, Iles IK. Advocacy in mental health nursing: an integrative review of the literature. *J Psychiatr Ment Health Nurs.* 2009;16:187–195.

Lown B, Kalet A. The clinician's experience: incorporating advocacy into the 20-minute encounter. In: Earp J, French E, Gilkey M, eds. *Patient Advocacy for Health Care Quality: Strategies for Achieving Patient-Centered Care.* Boston: Jones and Bartlett Publishers; 2008.

Manderson B, McMurray J, Piraino E, Stolee P. Navigation roles support chronically ill older adults through healthcare transitions: a systematic review of the literature. *Health Soc Care Community.* 2012;20:113–127.

Merriam-Webster. Available at www.merriam-webster.com. Accessed October 19, 2012.

Mitchell P, Hall L, Gaines M. A social compact for advancing team-based high-value health care. *Health Affairs Blog.* Available at http://healthaffairs.org/blog/2012/05/04/a-social-compact-for-advancing-team-based-high-value-health-care. Accessed October 19, 2012.

Nasca T, Philibert I, Brigham T, Flynn T. The next GME accreditation system—rationale and benefits. *N Engl J Med.* 2012;366:1051–1056.

National Center for Medical-Legal Partnership. Available at http://www.medical-legalpartnership.org. Accessed October 19, 2012.

Osler W. *Aequanimitas.* Philadelphia, PA: Blakiston; 1904.

Palfrey, J. *Child Health in America: Making a Difference Through Advocacy.* Baltimore, MD: Johns Hopkins University Press; 2006.

Palmer P. A new professional: the aims of education revisited. *Change.* November–December 2007. Available at http://www.changemag.org/Archives/Back%20Issues/November-December%202007/full-new-professional.html. Accessed October 19, 2012.

Robinson JC, Ginsburg PB. Consumer-driven health care: promise and performance. *Health Aff (Millwood).* 2009;28:w272–w281.

Rothman DJ. Medical professionalism: focusing on the real issues. *N Engl J Med.* 2000;342:1284–1286.

Schoen C, Osborn R, Squires D, Doty MM, Pierson R, Applebaum S. How health insurance design affects access to care and costs, by income, in eleven countries. *Health Aff (Millwood).* 2010;29:2323–2334.

Skocpol T. The political challenges that may undermine health reform. *Health Aff*. 2010;29(7):1288–1292.

Stern DT, Papadakis M. The developing physician—becoming a professional. *N Engl J Med*. 2006;355:1794–1799.

Wiktionary. Available at www.wiktionary.org. Accessed October 19, 2012.

Chapter 2

The Hippocratic Oath as an Example of Professional Conduct

HOWARD MARKEL

INTRODUCTION

All fields invested in the care of patients subscribe to ethical prin-
cipals that set the standard for their profession. As an historical
example, I propose exploring the origins and evolution of the best-
known canon of ethics in the health professions: the Hippocratic
Oath. Although it is an oath taken exclusively by physicians about
to enter medical practice and one that was written more than two
millennia ago, the changing interpretations of this text that have
resulted over time provide a useful framework for understanding
the conduct of contemporary health care professions.

Case History

The Time: The Age of Pericles, Euripides, Aeschylus,
Aristophanes, Socrates, and Plato, sometime around 400 B.C.

The Place: The Coan School of Medical Principles and
Practice on the Greek island of Kos.

The Scene: A group of students are gathered together in a
circle around their revered professor, Hippocrates. They are
about to complete their training and become members of the
medical profession. To make this transition, however, they

must first take a formal oath and enter into a binding covenant. Solemnly, they utter these now famous words:

I swear by Apollo Physician and Asclepius and Hygeia and Panacea and all the gods and goddesses, making them my witnesses, that I will fulfill according to my ability and judgement this oath and this covenant:

To hold him who has taught me this art as equal to my parents and to live my life in partnership with him, and if he is in need of money to give him a share of mine, and to regard his offspring as equal to my brothers in male lineage and to teach them this art—if they desire to learn it—without fee and covenant; to give a share of precepts and oral instruction and all the other learning to my sons and to the sons of him who has instructed me and to pupils who have signed the covenant and have taken an oath according to the medical law, but no one else.

I will apply dietetic measures for the benefit of the sick according to my ability and judgement; I will keep them from harm and injustice.

I will neither give a deadly drug to anybody who asked for it, nor will I make a suggestion to this effect. Similarly I will not give to a woman an abortive remedy. In purity and holiness I will guard my life and my art.

I will not use the knife, not even on sufferers from stone, but will withdraw in favor of such men as are engaged in this work.

Whatever houses I may visit, I will come for the benefit of the sick, remaining free of all intentional injustice, of all mischief and in particular of sexual relations with both female and male persons, be they free or slaves.

What I may see or hear in the course of the treatment or even outside of the treatment in regard to the life of men, which on no account one must spread abroad, I will keep to myself, holding such things shameful to be spoken about.

If I fulfill this oath and do not violate it, may it be granted to me to enjoy life and art, being honored with fame among all men for all time to come; if I transgress it and swear falsely, may the opposite of all this be my lot. (Edelstein, 1967)

DISCUSSION

As a medical historian, I have long enjoyed the Hippocratic Oath for its tradition of setting requirements that all physicians must subscribe to before they formally enter the medical profession. Yet, while the edicts handed down in the original version may seem a bit quaint, if not irrelevant, as a physician I make sure that every spring I dust off my bright yellow and black doctoral robe, my green, velvet-lined hood, and stiff, black mortarboard so that I can attend my medical school's commencement exercises. The purpose of this annual foray into pomp and circumstance goes well beyond applauding the achievements of the graduates. For me, commencement is the perfect opportunity to renew my vows, as it were, standing shoulder to shoulder with both newly minted doctors and like-minded colleagues. To be sure, elected officials are required to take an oath of office; members of the clergy in virtually every religion typically take vows before God; and even lawyers are accountable to a canon of ethical conduct and must take an oath to uphold the constitutions of their country and state. Yet none of these oaths have captured the public's imagination as firmly or for as long as the Hippocratic Oath.

Although many scholars dispute the exact authorship of the writings ascribed to Hippocrates (approximately 460–380 B.C.), at least for those who enjoy and appreciate the fruits of Western civilization, he remains revered as the "Father of Medicine." Hippocrates of Kos, "the Asclepiad," as he was referred to by Plato in *The Protagoras* and *The Phaedros*, was a disciple of the Coan school of medical thought that focused almost exclusively on the patient, in contrast to its chief rival, the Cnidian school, which articulated a reductionist focus on the classification of disease processes and the means of diagnosing them based upon an understanding and classification of local organ disturbances and symptom sets (Nuland, 1995).

Yet even if historians cannot precisely identify its author, the Hippocratic Oath is simultaneously one of the most cherished, protean, and misunderstood documents in the history of medicine. For example, modern interpreters often search the Oath in vain for general ethical principles to help guide the medical profession. Yet blind applications of an ancient oath to contemporary concerns discount the historical reality that the ideal physician of Hippocrates' era professed to be guided by Justice (as opposed to a moral code) as well as to identify himself as a reputable practitioner in competitive medical practices rife with bad behavior. Such a professional ethos is quite different from the concept of Charity and performing good works that guided the actions of medieval and Renaissance Christian physicians, let alone the modern-day social contract and the ethical and professional duties towards one's patients and the community at large that guide present-day doctors (Temkin, 1992; Jouanna, 1999).

Ironically, the Hippocratic Oath may also be one of the most misquoted documents in the history of medicine. For example, the medical profession's most treasured axiom, "First, do no harm" (a phrase translated from the Greek into Latin as *Primum non nocere*) is often mistakenly ascribed to the Oath, although it appears nowhere in that venerable pledge. What takers of the Oath do promise is: "I will keep them from harm and injustice." Hippocrates came closest to issuing the directive of "first, do no harm" in his treatise *Epidemics*, where the text informs the reader, "As to diseases, make a habit of two things—to help, or at least, to do no harm." (Hippocrates, "Epidemics," 1995).

Elsewhere, in treatises titled *Decorum, Law, Precepts,* and *The Physician,* Hippocrates describes a rigid code of behavior mandating that physicians be clean of person and dress, calm and honest, careful in how they give advice and recommendations, and maintain a serious yet empathetic demeanor. Similarly, the physician should "look healthy and as plump as nature intended him to be; for the common crowd consider those who are not of this excellent bodily condition, to be unable to take care of others." (Hippocrates, "Law," 1998; Hippocrates, "Precepts," 1995). Throughout his teachings, Hippocrates mandates that all doctors carefully observe and interview their patients. Detailed inquiries on the patient's complexion, pulse, temperature, aches and pains, diet, lifestyle, body movements and excretions, as well as his or her family and environmental history, are critical. As a fail-safe against a patient's potentially lying about or coloring his condition, the Greek physician suggested taking the patient's pulse during the interview. From all these encounters, the physician was also required to take careful notes and synthesize them into what we now know as a case history (Hippocrates, "Epidemics," 1995).

Many doctors practicing today are surprised to learn that the first recorded administration of the Hippocratic Oath in a medical school setting was at the University of Wittenberg in Germany in 1508, and that it did not become a standard part of a formal medical school graduation ceremony until 1804, when it was incorporated into the commencement exercises at Montpellier, France (Nutton, 1995). The custom spread in fits and starts on both sides of the Atlantic during the nineteenth century, but even well into the twentieth century, relatively few American physicians formally took the Oath. (Smith, 1996). Instead, these health professionals preferred subscribing to the code of ethical conduct first prescribed by the

American Medical Association in 1847, which has continued to be updated and rethought, albeit not widely read by most practicing physicians, to the present day (Baker et al., 1999).

According to a survey conducted for the Association of American Medical Colleges in 1928, only 19% of the medical schools in North America included the Oath in their commencement exercises (Carey, 1928). With the discovery of the atrocities that were committed in the name of medicine during World War II and the growing interest in bioethics in the succeeding decades, however, oath-taking began playing an increasing and prominent part in graduation ceremonies and, more broadly, the popular imagination. And while such goals were noble in their intent, those "rediscovering" the Hippocratic Oath in recent decades have rarely endeavored to historically contextualize this rich document, an essential task, not only for scholarly accuracy, but also to educate physicians about the long and ever-changing history of the medical profession (Smith, 1996).

Each spring, nearly every U.S. medical school administers some type of professional oath to its share of some 16,000 men and women who are eager to take possession of their medical degrees. Yet it is doubtful that Hippocrates would recognize most of the pledges that are anachronistically ascribed to him. Such revisionism is hardly unique to our era. Indeed, the tinkering with the Hippocratic Oath began soon after its first utterance and generally reflected the changing values, customs, and beliefs associated with the ethical practice of medicine. Some schools administer their own oaths, or prefer the Oath of Maimonides (Maimonides, 1917), or those written by other medical scholars. Still, the lack of consistency and varied attempts at political correctness evoked by many of these "oaths" complicate rather than explicate the endangered species called medical professionalism.

Consequently, there are stark differences between the promises made in the original version and the oaths sworn today. To take the most obvious example, few, if any, physicians now believe in the ancient Greek gods Apollo, Asclepius, Hygeia, and Panacea, and we, therefore, no longer pledge allegiance to this polytheistic pantheon. Although for many centuries between the Middle Ages and up to the twentieth century, oath-taking often invoked monotheistic Judeo-Christian beliefs, an allegiance to God and spirituality in general—regardless of its form—presently has a rather distant relationship with medical science: a "content analysis" of the oaths administered at 147 American and Canadian medical schools in 1993 showed that only 11% of the versions invoked a deity (Orr, et al., 1997).

In Hippocrates' day, the student made a binding vow to honor his teacher as he would his parents and to share financial and intellectual resources with his mentor and the mentor's family. Unfortunately for those of us engaged in medical education today, this pledge and its attendant remuneration by students to their senior professors has long since passed into disfavor. Even the relationships between attending physicians and the medical apprentices of the twenty-first century (e.g., interns, residents, and fellows) is currently in a great state of flux, from issues of work hours in the hospital during training, to the lifestyles demanded by medical trainees in contrast to the expectations of duty and professional commitment by their seniors.

There are two highly controversial vows in the original Hippocratic Oath that continue to be pondered and struggled with: the pledges never to participate in euthanasia or abortion. These prohibitions applied primarily to those identified as Hippocratic physicians, a medical sect that represented only a small minority of all self-proclaimed healers practicing in the ancient world. The Hippocratic physicians' reasons for refusing to participate in euthanasia may have been based on a philosophical or moral belief in preserving the sanctity of life, or simply a principled wish to avoid involvement in any act of assisted suicide, murder, or manslaughter. That said, there exists reliable historical documentation that many ancient Greeks and Romans, when confronted with terminal illness, preferred a quick, painless death by means of poison rather than letting nature take its course (Edelstein, 1967). Moreover, there were no laws in the ancient world against suicide, and it was not uncommon for physicians belonging to other medical sects to recommend, and even assist in, this option for a patient with an incurable disease. Similarly, abortion, typically effected by means of a pessary that induced premature labor, was widely practiced in both ancient Greece and during the reign of the Roman Empire. It was not until the Middle Ages that most Christian revisions of the Hippocratic Oath began to prohibit all abortive procedures. Not surprisingly, the contentious debate over both issues continues today, even though these relevant sections are simply omitted in most oaths administered by U.S. medical schools. As of 1993, only 14% of such oaths prohibited euthanasia, and only 8% prohibited abortion (Orr et al., 1997).

Another discarded relic is the vow never to "use the knife, not even on sufferers from the stone." In an era before antiseptic and aseptic surgery, anesthesia, and the scientific management of fluids, blood loss, and surgical shock, it was wise indeed to refer sufferers of these painful concretions of the bladder and kidney to those who "specialized" in their removal. Many healers in the ancient world focused their work specifically on kidney and bladder stones, others on cataract removal, and still others on the treatment of fractures and external injuries to the skin (Grmek, 1989).

That said, the *Hippocratic Corpus* is replete with suggestions on surgical interventions of the day. For example, the Hippocratic essay "In the Surgery" (Hippocrates, 1999) contains advice on how to conduct an operation, what sources of light to use, how one should stand when conducting an operation ("with the weight on one foot, not that on the side of the hand in use" and "with the height of the knees in the same relation to groins as when seated"), the proper length of the operator's fingernails ("neither to exceed nor come short of the fingertip"), and how to bandage a wound or set a fractured bone, among many other suggestions. Perhaps the best piece of Hippocratic surgical advice, one that remains cherished by modern surgeons, is to "practice all operations, performing them with each hand and with both together—for they are both alike—your object being to attain ability, grace, speed, painlessness, elegance, and readiness" (Hippocrates, 1999). Nevertheless, as recently as the end of the nineteenth century, even after the discovery of ether anesthesia, most surgical operations were treacherous affairs that carried a high risk of death by means of infection and sepsis (Markel, 2011). Consequently, the passage about "the knife" remains difficult to interpret. Historians have debated for centuries whether this vow bans all surgical procedures by the Hippocratic physicians because of their inherent danger, reflects the fact that many of these physicians considered surgery beneath their dignity and something best left to craftsmen, or represents a promise not to practice outside the bounds of one's abilities. In light of a mountain of conflicting evidence, it remains difficult to ascertain the precise origin and meaning of the clause prohibiting the use of the knife even for the "cutting of stone."

The Hippocratic physicians understood the importance of avoiding any type of sexual relationship with their patients, whether free or enslaved, yet only 3% the oaths administered by U.S. medical schools at the end of the twentieth century specifically prohibited such contact. On the other hand, virtually all the oaths administered today include the assurances that Hippocrates insisted were touchstones of the successful patient–doctor relationship: the promises of acting in the best interest of the patient and with strict confidentiality (Orr et al., 1997).

Often the additions made to the Hippocratic Oath in each era are as historically interesting as the deletions. Many of the oaths currently taken include vows not to alter one's practice on the basis of the patient's race, nationality, religion, sex, socioeconomic standing, or sexual orientation. Others include assurances of the physician's accountability to his or her patients, protection of the patients' autonomy, and informed consent or assistance with decision-making. In a very real sense, all these changes help make the act of oath-taking eternal, a process that constantly changes to accommodate and articulate changing views of medicine and society. Less common are clear, let alone universally accepted, approaches to family planning, patient privacy, and end-of-life issues. More recently, in a world of newly emerging infectious diseases, there has been wide controversy over whether or not a physician should put himself in harm's way when treating a contagious patient, a consideration that would never have occurred to the physician practicing before the era of vaccines and antibiotics. Those doctors of the past, of course, always put themselves in harm's way as part of their social contract with the patients they treated. Sadly, many of them became ill themselves with an infectious disease or died in "the line of fire."

CONCLUSIONS

Regardless of the language or provenance of the hundreds of texts collectively classified as "Hippocratic," on commencement day, the historian in me invariably takes a back seat to the physician. Personally, I have a distinct distaste for the bowdlerized, scrubbed, and amended versions that keep popping up each commencement day. Although the original Greek text uttered so long ago on the island of Kos is hopelessly out of date, I believe that there is great value in sticking to that text, with the clear understanding that the

Hippocratic Oath is a tradition rather than a recitation of Holy Scripture.

Despite occasional complaints questioning the relevance or purity of the oath-taking, this symbolic act is a tradition that is unlikely to become superannuated any time soon. It serves as a powerful reminder and declaration that we are all a part of something infinitely larger, older, and more important than a particular era, specialty, or institution. Given the myriad social quandaries facing almost every aspect of medicine in the twenty-first century, the need for physicians to make a formal warrant of diligent, moral, and ethical conduct and values in the service of their patients may be stronger than ever. How we come to an agreement on exactly what those terms are is an issue that lies at the very heart of every generation of physicians who come to grips with the daunting and ever-changing challenges facing the medical profession.

As every experienced doctor knows, the few minutes we spend giving voice to a professional oath are far easier than the years we must devote to its faithful execution. As Hippocrates famously said, "Life is short, the art long; opportunity fleeting, experience perilous, and the crisis difficult" (Hippocrates, "Aphorisms," 1998). Fortunately, the history (and present) of the medical profession suggests that we are capable of fulfilling this noble charge.

References

Baker RB, Caplan AL, Emanuel LL, Latham SR, eds. *The American Medical Ethics Revolution: How the AMA's Code of Ethics Has Transformed Physicians' Relationships to Patients, Professionals, and Society.* Baltimore: Johns Hopkins University Press; 1999.

Carey EJ. The formal use of the Hippocratic Oath for medical students at commencement exercises. *Bulletin of the Association of American Medical Colleges.* 1928;3:159–166.

Edelstein L. The Hippocratic Oath: Text, translation and interpretation. In: Temkin O, Temkin CL, eds. *Ancient Medicine: Selected Papers of Ludwig*

Edelstein. Baltimore: Johns Hopkins University Press; 1967:3–64; the Oath is found, in both Greek and English, on pp. 5–6.

Grmek MD. *Diseases in the Ancient World.* Trans. M Muellner, L Muellner. Baltimore: Johns Hopkins University Press; 1989:52–69.

Hippocrates. Epidemics, Book I, Section 11. In: *Hippocrates, Volume I.* Loeb Classical Library; trans. WHS Jones. Cambridge, MA: Harvard University Press; 1995:141–217; quote is from p. 165.

Hippocrates. Law; Decorum; The Physician. In: *Hippocrates, Volume II.* Loeb Classical Library; trans. WHS Jones. Cambridge, MA: Harvard University Press; 1998:255–315; quote is from The Physician, p. 311.

Hippocrates. Precepts. In: *Hippocrates, Volume I.* Loeb Classical Library; trans. WHS Jones. Cambridge, MA: Harvard University Press; 1995:303–333.

Hippocrates. In the Surgery. In: *Hippocrates, Volume III.* Loeb Classical Library; trans. ET Withington. Cambridge, MA: Harvard University Press; 1999:53–82; the quotes on how to stand while operating and the length of one's nails are from p. 61 and p. 63, respectively; the quote on "practicing all operations" also appears on p. 63.

Hippocrates. Aphorisms, Section 1:1. In: *Hippocrates, Volume IV.* Loeb Classical Library; trans. WHS Jones. Cambridge, MA: Harvard University Press; 1998:99.

Jouanna J. *Hippocrates.* Trans. MB Devoise. Baltimore: Johns Hopkins University Press; 1999.

Maimonides. The Oath and Prayer of Maimonides. Trans. H Freidenwald. *Bulletin of the Johns Hopkins Hospital.* 1917;28:260–261.

Markel H. *An Anatomy of Addiction: Sigmund Freud, William Halsted, and the Miracle Drug Cocaine.* New York: Pantheon/Alfred A. Knopf; 2011:94–95, 192–194, 290–291.

Nuland SB. *The totem of medicine: Hippocrates.* In: *Doctors: The Biography of Medicine.* New York: Vintage Books/Random House; 1995:3–30.

Nutton V. What's in an oath? *J R Coll Physicians London.* 1995;29:518–524.

Orr RD, Pang N, Pellegrino ED, Siegler M. Use of the Hippocratic Oath: a review of twentieth century practice and a content analysis of oaths administered in medical schools in the U.S. and Canada in 1993. *J Clin Ethics.* 1997;8:377–388.

Smith DC. The Hippocratic Oath and modern medicine. *J Hist Med Allied Sci.* 1996;51:484–500.

Temkin, O. *Hippocrates in a World of Pagans and Christians.* Baltimore: Johns Hopkins University Press; 1992.

Chapter 3

Professionalism and Politics
in the United Kingdom

CAROL BLACK AND
CYRIL CHANTLER

INTRODUCTION

Medicine has changed. It is now much more effective but also more complex and at times dangerous (Chantler, 1999). The dangers of modern medicine were documented in the United States by the Institute of Medicine in its landmark report "To Err Is Human" in 1999 (Kohn et al., 2000), and this was soon corroborated in other jurisdictions. In the United Kingdom several high-profile events called into question the quality and safety of some medical practice and led to a number of initiatives to promote quality in patient care, to reduce accidents, and to promote safety (Department of Health, 2006).

Physicians' primary and exclusive responsibility had been to and for their patients. That primary responsibility remains, but its nature has changed. The changes reflect strengthened emphasis on an individual's autonomy, society's readiness to question authority, and wide public access to information whose possession and interpretation were once accepted as the preserve of the professional.

Changes beyond the clinical encounter also have an impact on medical practice. Physicians now have contractual responsibilities to the organizations that employ them, and they may need to work within resource constraints imposed by the health care system they serve. Physicians work in teams that involve other health care professionals, and their capacity to do so successfully may be as important as their individual skills if excellent care is to be provided to their patients (West, 2010).

Obviously, physicians are required to practice within the law, but this requirement is insufficient to ensure good-quality patient care. Clinical governance requires an ethical and moral foundation. Successful practice requires trust between the physician and the patient, between members of the health care team, and between the profession and society. As the Cambridge moral philosopher Onora O'Neill has written, "Each of us and every profession and every institution needs to be trusted" (O'Neill, 2002). Trust is promoted not only by contracts and regulation but by the conscience of the practitioner. Indeed, regulation and some modern methods of seeking professional accountability can damage trust and are not an adequate substitute for it (O'Neill, 2002). The Scottish Enlightenment philosopher and economist Adam Smith pointed out in his book *A Theory of Moral Sentiments*, which is the companion book to *The Wealth of Nations*, that conscience or a sense of duty to others is as important as the possibility of financial gain in motivating human behavior. Conscience is not just an intellectual concept; it needs to find expression in everyday behavior and in relationships with others. Its importance should be recognized in the values of the organizations in which we work and hopefully in the societies in which we live.

In the United Kingdom over the last decade, there have been profound changes in the regulation of physicians, both in terms of contracts with the main employer, the National Health Service (NHS), and in the requirements of the profession's own regulator, the General Medical Council (GMC). Many of these initiatives have stemmed from the physicians themselves. In this respect, the profession has engaged with itself and with society in asking what modern medical professionalism means, how can it be better understood, how can it be developed, and how can it be ensured (Royal College of Physicians, 2005). Standards for clinical practice in the United Kingdom are the responsibility of the Royal Colleges that cover all specialties, including general practice and the family doctor service.

The employer and the state have an interest in standards of practice and ensuring patient safety and a high-quality service. This interest is exercised directly through contracts of employment, through the organization of the service, and by its influence on the main regulator, the GMC, and its accountability to Parliament. Conscience and professionalism as well as contractual issues are therefore interwoven in the standards set by the Royal Colleges, by the GMC, and by the state. Trust can only be promoted if these arrangements are coordinated and comprehensive. Many changes have been introduced in recent years to modernize the system and to ensure that it works to provide a safe and effective service to patients.

The purpose of this chapter is to review these changes from the perspective of the Medical Royal Colleges, particularly the Royal College of Physicians (RCP), the GMC, and the NHS, and the Government through the Department of Health (DH).

PROFESSIONALISM AND THE MEDICAL ROYAL COLLEGES

The Medical Royal Colleges and their Faculties are independent national professional membership bodies. Their aims and activities have to do with the protection and improvement of health, prevention of disease, and the improvement of health care. They work to achieve these aims by promoting the best possible performance against the highest standards in medical education and training, the practice of medicine, academic medicine, and research in the ways services are delivered and in the exercise of medical professionalism. They also take responsibility to inform and, where possible, to influence health policy development and implementation. The charters and bylaws of individual Colleges put these things in their own ways, to which each of them brings deep knowledge of the specialized areas of medicine that lie within their remit.

The statutory regulatory bodies, parliamentarians and government, and health service organizations look to and often work with the Colleges and Faculties for authoritative opinion and advice in fulfilling their own duties and functions.

The Academy of Medical Royal Colleges brings the Colleges and their Faculties together with the primary purpose of supporting and promoting their work and providing a forum for discussion and collaboration between them. It provides a collective voice on behalf of medical collegiate bodies of the United Kingdom, where it is agreed that a collective approach is appropriate (Academy of Medical Royal Colleges website, accessed June 23, 2012). For many years, by virtue of its standing and influence, the Royal College of Physicians has taken a leading professional role in responding to the flow of societal changes that have implications for healthcare, medical professional institutions, and for medical practice (Royal College of Physicians website, accessed June 23, 2012).

The publication in 2002 of "Medical Professionalism in the New Millennium: A Physicians' Charter," prepared by the American Board of Internal Medicine Foundation, the American College of Physicians/American Society of Internal Medicine, and the European Federation of Internal Medicine, served to heighten discussion on patient care and professionalism in the United Kingdom.

In 2004, The King's Fund, an independent charitable foundation working for better health, published a discussion paper, "On
Being a Doctor." Redefining medical professionalism for better
patient care (Rosen and Dewar, 2004), it also drew attention to
challenges arising from the changing conditions of practice and the
expectations of patients, government, and health service managers.
The paper commented that, while physicians remain highly trusted,
the profession as a whole needed to demonstrate better its overrid-
ing duty to serve patients' interests and to show that it can respond
to changing public and political expectations. It concluded that that
a modern definition of medical professionalism was needed.

Earlier that year, following a seminar on professionalism, the
Royal College of Physicians had decided to answer this need. The
College, well aware that the issues were of wide public concern and
interest, assembled a working party whose membership extended
far beyond the College and the profession. It began its task with the
assumption that at the heart of good medical care is a set of values,
attitudes, and behaviors called *medical professionalism*. The aim was
to discover what is understood by the concept of medical professionalism today, to formulate a description that could command
wide recognition and support, and to make recommendations to
help shape a new medical professionalism as a valued force in the
life of our society in the United Kingdom.

The working party took oral evidence from 19 witnesses, all
eminent in their own fields. It received over 100 written responses
to a set of questions about medical professionalism, commissioned
a questionnaire and focus groups, drew on peer-reviewed literature,
and took additional soundings from a broad range of medical and
lay opinion. This evidence provided the substance of the working
party's deliberations and the basis of its report.

The report was published in 2005 (Royal College of Physicians,
2005). Its recommendations were for a new, strengthened form of

medical professionalism, valid for the current time, to maintain trust and confidence in physicians and their part in our system of health care. They gave renewed emphasis to qualities that must endure, discarding those that have become outdated, and brought in new aspects that recognized the extended responsibilities of physicians today.

The report defined medicine as a vocation in which a physician's knowledge, clinical skills, and judgement are put to the service of protecting and restoring human well-being. This purpose is to be realized through a partnership between patient and physician, one based on mutual respect, individual responsibility, and appropriate accountability. It reaffirmed the commitment to integrity, compassion, altruism, continuous improvement, and excellence, and working in partnership with members of the wider health care team.

The report again affirmed that medical professionalism today incurs many other duties and responsibilities. They include responsibilities to the institutions in which physicians work; and, more widely, the system within which health care is provided. Such corporate responsibility, calling for leadership and partnership with others, had not been a strong feature of the professional ethos hitherto. It was given great emphasis in the report, and a range of actions has been taken to remedy this shortcoming. Other responsibilities for a modern physician might include encouraging justice in health care provision, functioning as public health professionals to reduce the burden of chronic disease, practicing medicine with a deep awareness of the social determinants of health, and facilitating the introduction of new systems of care.

The report "Doctors in Society" (Royal College of Physicians, 2005) was not for the profession and its institutions alone. The recommendations called for responsible engagement, drawing in a well-informed public alongside the medical profession, together with the national agencies that have an essential part in bringing about the steps necessary. Although what was done seems now clear enough, the report was in several ways a radical departure from what had gone on before, showing a determination to draw the profession more closely into true partnerships with every element of our society involved in health care and its provision and delivery.

In 2008, working together, the Royal College and the King's Fund undertook national consultations, which included asking physicians to reflect on their own future and the future of medical professionalism. Their joint report, "Understanding Doctors: Harnessing Professionalism" (Levenson, 2008), brought together the views of physicians, patients, family caregivers, nurses and allied health professionals, NHS managers, and medical students on issues of critical importance to the day-to-day practice of medicine, to improving standards, to facilitating team working, and to putting the needs of patients at the forefront of health care delivery.

None disputed the Royal College of Physicians' definition of "medical professionalism" as a set of values, behaviors, and relationships that underpins the trust the public has in physicians. Indeed, there was considerable optimism that such a professionalism was alive and well. However, it was widely acknowledged that physicians, individually and collectively, needed to reconsider how these values should be put into practice in a rapidly changing society.

Meanwhile, in 2008, coinciding with marking 150 years of the Medical Act, the medical profession in the United Kingdom reached a consensus on the role of the physician (Medical Schools Council, 2008). This was a response to the need to provide clarity on the role in order to inform medical education, training, and workforce planning. The consensus statement set out the core attributes necessary to merit the trust of patients, and the personal qualities that are the foundations of those attributes. It thus reinforced the special place of medical professionalism. The statement again affirmed that, not withstanding the primacy of the individual physician–patient relationship, physicians also have obligatory roles in the stewardship of the health care system. This stewardship carries wider duties and responsibilities, and further accountability.

Importantly, the consensus statement was supported formally by the Chief Medical Officers of England, Scotland, Wales, and Northern Ireland; the Academy of Medical Royal Colleges; the Association of UK University Hospitals; the British Medical Association; Council of Postgraduate Medical Deans (COPMeD—a UK-wide organization that represents the Postgraduate Deans and Deaneries); the GMC; the King's Fund; the Medical Schools Council; NHS Employers; and PMETB (the Postgraduate Medical Education and Training Board, now merged with the GMC).

REGULATION AND THE GENERAL MEDICAL COUNCIL (GMC)

The GMC was established in 1858 by an Act of Parliament following a campaign by allopathic practitioners for them to be distinguished from other health practitioners who were less well qualified (Irvine, 2006). The Act established a register of qualified physicians. The original council had 24 members, all medical practitioners, though a lay member was appointed in 1926 to represent patient interests. As has been observed, self-regulation represents a contract between the profession and the state whereby the profession promises the public that they will protect them from bad physicians in return for a substantial degree of autonomy to regulate its own affairs (Irvine, 2006).

Unfortunately the history of the GMC does not inspire confidence; it has been reorganized many times, with major changes being introduced in 1980 when the council was expanded to

93 members, seven of them laymen, with a majority of the medical members being elected by the profession as a whole. At that time, the council was responsible for four functions: to register physicians, to regulate basic medical education, to deal with fitness to practice, and to provide advice on professional standards and ethics.

While the GMC holds the ultimate sanction in that it can, after due process, remove a physician from the register and therefore from practicing, its main function is or should be to promote professionalism; thus it operates more in the realm of conscience than contract.

In the early 1990s, the GMC Standards Committee began to develop a standards-based model for medical licensure. As the then-chairman of the Standards Committee, Donald Irvine, has written, the objective was to unify the profession around a set of generic duties and attributes that both the profession and the public thought were important in a good physician (Irvine, 2006). This code of practice (GMC, 2006; Chantler and Ashton, 2009) was first published in 1995, has been regularly updated, and is now the basis for registration and lies at the heart of the new systems being introduced to revalidate at regular intervals a physician's fitness to practice. The pamphlet, which is sent to all physicians and medical students, starts with a one-page summary that sets out clearly the duties a physician owes to a patient and to society; emphasizing that practice is a privilege, not a right. A number of medical schools use the "Duties of a Doctor" as set out in the document as a spoken commitment, a modern-day Hippocratic oath, during the graduation ceremony. "Good Medical Practice" (GMC, 2006) is now established as a statement of generic medical standards capable of being operationalized into the governance of everyday clinical practice (Irvine, 2006). As such, it lies at the heart of modern professionalism.

Unfortunately, the Council with 93 members elected/appointed in 1979 did not prove fit for purpose. Complaints were made by the public, the media, and politicians that it was too physician-dominated and was failing to protect the public from unsafe practice. Physicians anxious for reform joined the chorus of criticism, and eventually, following a number of public scandals, a new and smaller council with 24 members, half of them laymen, was established in 2003. In 1999 the GMC decided that all physicians in active practice should have their practice evaluated regularly to ensure they were up to date and fit to practice. While the GMC is responsible for generic standards of practice, the standards for specialist practice are set by the Royal Colleges (see above), and they are therefore intimately involved in revalidation or recertification.

One of the concerns both about the generic standards and the concept of the standards to be applied to regular recertification has been the scope of regulation. Should the regulator set standards for personal behavior outside clinical practice, including the notion of not bringing the profession into disrepute? Should its code include the regulation of physicians in managerial positions or those engaged with research? Is the profession setting standards that are higher than the law requires for physicians as compared to others undertaking similar activities? Should they be held to account for the efficiency of their practice as well as its safety and effectiveness (Chantler and Ashton, 2009)? In these respects, the question arises as to whether these and similar questions are more a matter for contract than conscience or professional standards.

Despite recertification being practiced in other countries such as the United States, and that it had been shown to improve standards of care (Sutherland and Leatherman, 2006), its introduction in the United Kingdom has proven to be controversial. A judicial inquiry in 2004—concerning a notorious case of a physician who became a serial killer—cast serious doubt on the effectiveness of the GMC's proposals for revalidation every five years. The report was highly critical of the culture, membership, methods of working, and governance of the GMC, which had failed to implement its own recommendations made in 2001 (Smith, 2004); not least because of opposition from the profession. Accordingly, the government asked the Chief Medical Officer to review the workings of the GMC and to advise about how an effective system of revalidation should be ensured.

ROLE OF GOVERNMENT

Recognition that modern health can be dangerous has led to a focus on clinical governance. The term *clinical governance* was introduced in 1998 as part of the government's response to increasing public disquiet about safety in the NHS following a number of examples of poor practice leading to harm to patients (Department of Health, 1998). It was represented as the clinical equivalent of corporate governance in the field of commerce and was defined as "a system through which NHS organizations are accountable for continuously improving the quality of their services and safeguarding high standards of care by creating an environment in which excellence in clinical care will flourish" (Scally and Donaldson, 1998). The focus was to be on quality, and the development of clinical standards to be applied to care throughout the NHS. Later, these policies were supplemented by the creation of the National Patient Safety Agency (National Patient Safety Agency website, accessed 2012), This followed a report from the Chief Medical Officer entitled "An Organization with a Memory" (Department of Health, 2000) that analyzed the number of serious mishaps leading to death and harm which occurred each year in the NHS; indeed it was estimated that around 10% of all hospital admissions were complicated by adverse avoidable events.

It is obvious from this analysis that government and politicians representing the people have had an increasing role over the last few years both in regulating the practice of medicine and in the regulation of clinical practitioners, not least, physicians. We regret that it has to be acknowledged that the profession's own regulatory body did not respond adequately to public concern and the mounting evidence that unsafe practice was occurring. This led to the Department of Health's issuing new guidance to the GMC in 2006 (Department of Health, 2006). In spite of this, and the clear determination of the then-government that revalidation should be mandatory, over 13 years after it was first proposed by the then-president of the GMC, it has not yet started. The GMC is formally accountable to the British Parliament, not the government, and a recent report by the Parliamentary Health Committee makes it clear that they expected the process to start in 2012 (House of Commons, 2011).

The tortuous history of revalidation or recertification of physicians and the role the state has had to take to improve clinical governance, including placing an obligation to cooperate with its procedures into contracts of employment, might be regarded as a failure of professionalism by the profession. This is partly true, but it is also true that the GMC and the specialist Royal Colleges can be proud of their leadership in setting standards for practice and behavior and honesty. The Royal College of Physicians in particular has led the debate on the importance of professionalism, and the hope for the future is that a renaissance of professionalism will mean that the role of conscience will once more assume dominance over contract and create the trust that is so essential for clinical practice.

CONCLUSION

The standing of the medical profession is measured in a plain and vivid way: it is seen in the trust and confidence patients and the public have in physicians and their part in our system of health care. Today that trust and confidence are tempered by reference to standards—a mantra of explicit standards, widely disseminated and reinforced. They are standards of knowledge, skills, experience, attitudes, conduct, and the values judged necessary for continuing practice. They are standards against which each professional is called to account, and in future will be called regularly to account through the processes of revalidation.

Regulation and professionalism explore many shared concerns, but they come from different directions, often with different emphases. Regulation of professional action can be very wide-ranging, more extensive, and sometimes less sharply defined than that undertaken by statutory professional regulatory bodies. Regulation also comes, for example, from central and local priorities, authoritative guidance, and contracts of employment. The interaction of each of these modes of regulation with the professional ethos is, perhaps, no less important than the interaction with the statutory bodies.

There are tensions, familiar to all, between the beliefs, aims, wishes, ambitions, demands, and motives of different stakeholders. Such tensions are found in any vigorous society. They are the substance of ethical debate. Clinical practice is not conducted in isolation. Professional standards and professional behavior must, within accepted ethical boundaries, be more or less in tune with prevailing values and expectations. But that does not mean acquiescence in claims or actions that are harmful, selfish, or unfair, or promises to meet expectations that are pitched unreasonably high.

Problems arise when political or managerial differences about the policies adopted or the manner of implementation run counter to the values of professionalism. Their resolution demands candid, constructive dialogue based on respect and trust. Both have been severely tested in recent times.

It is essential that government, in its zeal for reform, acknowledges the ethos of our medical professional institutions and the goals to which that professionalism is directed. Those most closely involved in policy making, development, and implementation must learn to put their trust in clinicians. This means more than willingness to share openly in their deliberations and decision-making processes: it means entrusting clinicians with both the authority and responsibility to implement change.

The values of medical professionalism and of society, and the aims of government to improve the quality and safety and the clinical and cost-effectiveness of care, are not dissimilar. They should reinforce each other. We are increasingly confident that the firm commitment of our professional bodies, alongside developments in professional education and training in the wake of regulatory reform, will protect and strengthen the new professionalism, helping it to develop and flourish.

References

Academy of Medical Royal Colleges. *Academy Strategic Plan 2012–2015.* Available at http://www.aomrc.org.uk/. Accessed June 23, 2012.
Chantler C. The role and education of doctors in the delivery of health care. *Lancet.* 1999;353(9159):1178–1181.
Chantler C, Ashton R. The purpose and limits to professional self-regulation. *JAMA.* 2009;302(18):2032–2033.
Department of Health. *A First Class Service: Quality in the NHS.* London: The Stationery Office; 1998.
Department of Health. *An Organization with a Memory.* London: The Stationery Office; 2000.
Department of Health. *Good Doctors, Safer Patients.* London: Crown; 2006.
GMC. Good Medical Practice, 2006; available at http://www.gmc-uk.org/guidance/good_medical_practice/good_doctors.asp. Accessed June 23, 2012.
House of Commons Health Committee. *Revalidation of Doctors.* London: The Stationery Office; 2011.
Irvine D. A short history of the General Medical Council. *Med Educ.* 2006; 40(3):202–211.

Kohn LT, Corrigan JM, Donaldson MS. *To Err Is Human: Building a Safer Health System*. Washington, DC: National Academy Press; 2000; available at http://www.nap.edu/openbook.php?isbn=0309068371.

Levenson R, Dewar S, Shepherd May S. *Understanding Doctors: Harnessing Professionalism*. London: Kings Fund and Royal College of Physicians; 2008.

Medical professionalism in the new millennium: a physicians' charter. *Lancet*. 2002;359(9305):520–522.

Medical Schools Council. Consensus Statement on the Role of the Doctor, 2008; available at http://www.medschools.ac.uk. Accessed June 23, 2012.

National Patient Safety Agency. www.npsa.nhs.uk/corporate/. Accessed June 20, 2012.

O'Neill O. *A Question of Trust*. Reith Lectures; London, 2002.

Rosen R, Dewar S. *On Being a Doctor: Redefining Medical Professionalism for Better Patient Care*. London: King's Fund; 2004.

Royal College of Physicians. http://www.rcplondon.ac.uk/. Accessed June 23, 2012.

Royal College of Physicians. *Doctors in Society, Medical Professionalism in a Changing World*. London: Royal College of Physicians; 2005.

Scally G, Donaldson LJ. The NHS's 50th anniversary. Clinical governance and the drive for quality improvement in the new NHS in England. *BMJ*. 998;317(7150):61–65.

Smith J. *The Shipman Inquiry. Fifth Report; Safeguarding Patients: Lessons from the Past—Proposals for the Future*. London: The Stationery Office; 2004.

Sutherland K, Leatherman S. Does certification improve medical standards? *BMJ*. 2006;333(7565):439–441.

West M. *Management and Leadership in Challenging Times*. Health Service Research Network; 2010. Available at http://www.nhsconfed.org/Documents/Michael%20West.9%20Sept%20Presentation%20pdf.pdf. Accesseed June 23, 2012.

Chapter 4

The Role of Specialty Boards in Promoting Professionalism

The Case of the American Board of Internal Medicine

CLARENCE H. BRADDOCK III,
ERIC S. HOLMBOE, AND CHRISTINE K. CASSEL

HISTORY OF THE AMERICAN BOARD OF INTERNAL MEDICINE

The American Board of Internal Medicine (ABIM) and the ABIM Foundation were born from the impetus of the medical profession to establish credible standards for physician specialists to serve the public. Established in 1936, the ABIM followed the example of several surgical specialties—as a creation of the American Medical Association (AMA) and the medical specialty society, in this case the American College of Physicians (ACP)—to create a separate and independent organization to set standards for what it meant to be a board-certified internist. In the founding documents from this period, the ACP and AMA acknowledged that, in order for the public to be confident in the designations of board certification, the board issuing those credentials must be separate from the membership societies in order to mitigate political pressures that might emerge during the standard-setting process.

The mission of ABIM is "to enhance the quality of health care by certifying internists and subspecialists who demonstrate the knowledge, skills, and attitudes essential for excellent patient care." The Board's tagline, "Of the profession, for the public," is intended to codify a commitment to maintaining the social contract through standards of excellence. Thus, even the founding of these organizations has at its core a responsibility primarily to the public as part of the definition of professionalism.

THE MODERN CONTEXT: PROFESSIONALISM AS ACCOUNTABILITY

There has long been a tension among multiple stakeholders in their understanding of the term *professionalism*. While physicians think of professionalism as inherently a good thing and as inherently doing the right thing, the public sometimes views it as a "smokescreen" behind which the profession can hold authority for standards and consider the patient's interest from a paternalistic perspective, but believing that the public is not expert enough to determine professional standards. The modern world has brought us to a different place, where public input and patient views of standards of care are understood to be an important component of health care quality. Sometimes this is called "accountability" in a marketplace sense, meaning that physicians and other health care professionals need to be accountable to the people who pay the bill, including patients, their families, the employers who provide insurance, and the payers; that is, the private insurance companies and the government through Medicare/Medicaid and other programs.

The profession has responded to the need for accountability by strengthening its independent standard-setting process of board certification. This has meant moving from board certification's signifying that the holder has passed an exam of knowledge at the end of his or her training and resulting in a lifetime certification, to the need for physicians to episodically demonstrate that they keep up with the standards known as "Maintenance of Certification" or MOC. All 24 specialties of the American Board of Medical Specialties (ABMS) boards have now agreed to a periodic reexamination of physicians' knowledge as well as demonstration of their performance in practice.

The ideal of professionalism has evolved to encompass the ultimate link with public accountability. Board certification and MOC now represent a tangible expression of this accountability. Over time, we expect that the movement of accountability and the movement of professionalism will increasingly more closely align with each other to reduce the burden of redundant measures on physicians and to more accurately signify to patients and consumers the reliability, ability, and performance of physician professionals. Where is professionalism in this complex tangle of measurement and accountability? Professionalism is demonstrated by the physician's willingness to take part in these accountability activities— ranging from MOC, to public reporting, to specialty boards and societies embracing the importance of that agenda.

THE WORK OF ABIM AND THE ABIM
FOUNDATION ON PROFESSIONALISM

Most definitions of professionalism acknowledge in some form the "social contract" that forms part of its foundation. In its simplest form, the social contract is a hypothetical promise between the profession and society. In exchange for its special status and the special privileges given to it by society as part of this contract, the profession makes certain commitments, among them fidelity, the promise to act on behalf of patients, and the commitment to self-regulation, to exercise due diligence to assure that all practitioners are qualified to serve.

From its inception, the ABIM demonstrated its commitment to professionalism, primarily through the board-certification process. Although the format and content of this process changed over the decades, board certification remained the foundational element of ABIM's exercise of self-regulation of professional competence. Over time, the extent of the breadth and depth of this on behalf of professionalism has expanded.

Emphasizing Humanistic Values in Certification

In the 1980s, ABIM identified "humanistic qualities" as a formal component of clinical competence and as a requirement for certification. As part of its standards for initial certification, ABIM began requiring residency and fellowship programs to evaluate trainees' professionalism and moral and ethical behavior on an annual basis. Failure to achieve a satisfactory rating in any of these domains disqualifies the trainee from advancing in training or attaining certification until he or she successfully remediates the deficiencies, and that can require an entire year of additional training. The ABIM Subcommittee on Humanistic Qualities created a standardized definition of these qualities—integrity, respect, and compassion— and supported research to demonstrate that these attributes could be evaluated and documented in the training environment with the support of each residency and subspecialty program director and the use of an effective evaluation system (*Guide to Awareness*, 1994).

Recertification and Maintenance of Certification

Faced with growing challenges to the validity of lifetime board certification, in 1990 ABIM limited all certifications in its specialties and subspecialties to ten years' duration. This recertification requirement signaled to internists and the public that there would be accountability for a commitment to lifelong learning and improvement through assessment. The original pillars of recertification were a self-evaluation process (SEP), a clinical competence assessment, and a secure exam. Over the past two decades, recertification has evolved both in name—to "continuous professional development" in 2000, and now "Maintenance of Certification" (MOC)—and in sophistication and rigor.

MOC in its current form has four parts:

- *Part I:* Maintenance of Licensure and Professional Standing: To maintain certification, the physician must hold and maintain a valid, unrestricted medical license.
- *Part II:* Assessment of Medical Knowledge: The physician demonstrates a commitment to lifelong learning through participation in educational activities that include some element of self-assessment.
- *Part III:* Demonstration of Cognitive Expertise: The physician must demonstrate this by performance on a secure exam.
- *Part IV:* Assessment of Performance in Practice: The physician must engage in self-assessment of practice performance, include reflecting on data and creating an improvement plan.

In its current form, MOC has become a much more sophisticated process, and has begun to gain the recognition and respect of the world outside the discipline. For example, the Center for Medicare and Medicaid Services (CMS) is actively considering how to credit active participation in MOC in its "Physician Quality Reporting Initiative" (PQRI) program.

On the horizon is "Continuous MOC" (CMOC), which adds new requirements for assessment of practitioners' knowledge regarding patient safety, and feedback from patients gathered from patient surveys. Also, CMOC moves the MOC requirements from infrequent burst of activity (every 10 years) to a more continuous cycle of activity; that is, every two years.

Project Professionalism

In 1990, the ABIM launched an initiative to further support professional and humanistic values as a key component of the evaluation of competence. This initiative, *Project Professionalism,* had four main goals:

(1) Define professionalism;
(2) Raise the concept of professionalism in the consciousness of all within internal medicine;
(3) Provide a means for program directors to inculcate the concepts of professionalism within their training programs; and
(4) Develop strategies for assessing the professionalism of residents and subspecialty fellows during training.

Project Professionalism was guided by a task force of experts in residency training, education, and professionalism. The group created a set of program requirements for internal medicine training that were adopted by the Internal Medicine Residency Review Committee (RRC) in 2000, a set of educational resources, and a series of assessment tools to aid program directors in both formative and summative assessment of performance in professionalism and ethical conduct.

ABIM Foundation and the "Physicians' Charter"

In 1999, the ABIM board of directors created a foundation whose board included members of the abim (in addition to the ibim board members. Its mission is the promotion of professionalism, quality of care, and the physician's role in advancing quality of care. An early activity of the ABIM Foundation, with the ACP Foundation and the European Federation of Internal Medicine, produced a charter to provide physicians in the twenty-first century with guideposts for ethical professionalism in the complex modern world (ABIM Foundation, 2002). The traditional codes of ethics stemming from Hippocrates, Maimonides, and other iconic medical voices from thousands of years ago emphasize physicians' dedication to the well-being of patients. This fundamental goal remains unchanged. But the modern environment of medicine has new challenges, including market pressures and the increasing role of engaged and empowered patients. "The Physician's Charter on Professionalism" reflects these realities and was published simultaneously in the *Annals of Internal Medicine* and the *Lancet*. It is worth noting how unusual it is for any medical editor to agree to simultaneously publish the exact same article in two journals, an indication of the uniqueness and importance of this charter.

The charter is based on three principles: patient autonomy, patient well-being, and social justice. Based on these principles, the authors derived 10 commitments that ethical physicians in the twenty-first century should endorse:

- Professional competence
- Honesty with patients
- Patient confidentiality
- Maintaining appropriate relations with patients
- Improving quality of care
- Improving access to care
- A just distribution of finite resources
- Scientific knowledge
- Maintaining trust by managing conflicts of interest
- Professional responsibilities

This list of commitments includes some things that are very familiar and traditional, tying back to the original Hippocratic tradition such as the primacy of patient care and welfare, but some commitments reflect modern challenges and modern realities such as avoiding conflicts of interest, and being honest with patients.

ABIM Foundation: Putting the Charter into Practice

After the publication of the charter and its widespread adoption throughout medical education and internationally, the ABIM began focusing on ways to operationalize or implement aspects of the charter. The list of 10 commitments has become a kind of checklist for the Board when it and the Foundation select areas of focus.

The first issue that the Foundation took on was the question of conflict of interest with industry sources of influence on physicians' prescribing activities, reviewing evidence about the ways in which gifts and contributions from industry sources could subliminally and unconsciously affect prescribing behavior of physicians in training (Brennan, 2006). The Foundation's strong recommendation was to discontinue widely accepted practices such as pharmaceutical industry sponsorship of residency training-program lunches, the giving of gifts ranging from stethoscopes to minor items such as pens and notepads, and paying faculty for speeches. The publication of this document stimulated reflection within the academic medical world. Some organizations (such Kaiser Permanente) had already established a practice of not allowing industry influence into the training center or areas of physician practice. But in medical schools always struggling for financial resources to support educational activities, these perquisites, minor as they were, proved difficult to forego. However, prompted by this report and wider dialogue on this issue, many academic centers stepped forward and changed those practices. In the leadership of this were organizations such as the University of Pennsylvania and Stanford—major teaching institutions. For example, as of 2012, 81 medical schools had publicly gone on record to eliminate the industry-sponsored gifts and meals in their training programs. (AMSA Scorecard, 2012)

In 2007, the ABIM Foundation sponsored a forum entitled "Coordination of Care: Missed Opportunity," to which it invited more than 120 health care leaders to identify successful models, organizational strategies, and structural and financial changes needed for the health care system to improve care coordination. In this convening role, the Foundation was able to launch a set of activities to advance care coordination, including publication of an important paper and work with the Physician Consortium for Performance Improvement (PCPI) in developing metrics for care coordination (Bodenheimer, 2008).

Following a similar approach, the ABIM Foundation has convened a series of meetings over the ensuing years: "From Rhetoric to Reality: Advancing Patient-Centered Care" in 2008; "Achieving Equity, Affordability and Quality: The Indispensable Role of Payment Reform" in 2009; and "Transforming Medical Education and Training: Meeting the Needs of Patients and Society" in 2010. All led to tangible impacts on health care and on attitudes of the profession. Each served as an effective and impactful expression of parts of the Physician Charter.

The Foundation also worked to refine the definition of *professionalism*. After sponsoring a multi-stakeholder conference with representatives from the public, payers, government agencies, physician specialty societies, and nursing, ABIM Foundation formed the Professionalism Task Force. The Task Force explored the relationship between physician behaviors and the organizational and environmental context in which care is delivered, resulting in proposed model of professionalism (Lesser et al., 2010).

In 2011, the ABIM Foundation elected to refocus its efforts on the area of stewardship of scarce medical resources in an environment where the rising costs of care in the United States have distorted numerous aspects of the economy, creating a major drag on economic productivity of businesses and adding an enormous burden to individual patients and families with the cost of insurance premiums, out-of-pocket costs, or the very real costs of being uninsured in an environment where insurance is increasingly unaffordable. In addition, the challenging economic times of global recession have led the government to realize that the federal support of Medicare and Medicaid and other federal health care programs as they continue to rise in cost are also unsustainable. In this environment, the role of the physician is controversial and not well articulated.

In 2012, the Foundation launched the "Choosing Wisely" campaign, engaging the medical specialty societies to identify tests and treatments susceptible to overuse in their areas, and partnering with consumer organizations led by Consumers Union to disseminate information about the risk and expense of over-treatment and over-testing for consumers (Cassel and Guest, 2010). This campaign has been met with extraordinary response from all sectors in health care and the general public. Many journalists have commented that what is truly remarkable and newsworthy about this campaign is the willingness of specialty societies (at this point, more than 20) to step forward and acknowledge that there are areas in their specialty that have been overused and to promote the idea of reducing the use of procedures that are potentially lucrative for them. This is an important marker of professionalism and a clear effort to put the patient first. It is also an important harbinger of the need to change the environment and context of health care to promote professionalism rather than be a barrier to professionalism (Cassel and Jain, 2012). For example, changing the financing and payment procedures could provide physicians with economic rewards for more prudent prescribing, rather than economic penalties.

Promoting Professionalism Through Research on Assessment

ABIM has also advanced the field of professionalism through research and scholarship. The ABIM recognized the need for rigorous and meaningful assessment of performance and professionalism beginning in the late 1980s. The work initially focused on assessment of humanism and professional behaviors that led to the development of a patient survey, a peer survey, and a nursing survey (Ramsey et al., 1993; Weinrich et al., 1993). This early research demonstrated that a meaningful and reliable assessment of the competencies of professionalism and interpersonal and communication skills was possible. Furthermore, pioneering work with the ABIM found that peer ratings correlated with important metrics of competence, such as medical knowledge, and that such ratings could provide valuable feedback to physicians on these important but "softer" skills (Ramsey et al., 1993). This early work in performance-based assessment around professionalism and communication skills ultimately led to the development of a combined peer-patient assessment module that was introduced as part of the ABIM continuous professional development programs (later known as MOC) in the late 1990s.

In 2006, the ABIM added the requirement to evaluate performance in practice as part of the MOC program, and the peer-patient module was an option physicians could use to obtain valuable feedback for their improvement plan. Several thousand physicians chose this module to meet the evaluation-of-performance requirement and reported high levels of satisfaction with the experience. The module also was adapted by many others both in the United States and abroad for use in training programs.

Research demonstrated the module possessed good psychometric properties, including validity, and showed that it could detect outlier physicians with poor professionalism and communication skills (Lipner et al., 2002). A group of gastroenterologists chose the peer component of the survey as part of their pay-for-performance program in Rochester, New York (H. Beckman, personal communication). ABIM's early experience with a multi-source feedback approach was replicated by others outside the United States, most notably in Alberta, Canada, where a novel multi-source feedback instrument that includes patient, peer, and healthcare colleague surveys has become a core component of the physician assessment review program for the province (Hall and Lewkonia, 1999).

Despite the early success of the peer-patient module, the survey was limited in the number of questions asked of raters. In 2010, the peer and patient module was formally replaced by a new group of survey modules that expanded the number of domains of professional behavior that could be evaluated. These new modules include several versions of the Consumer Assessment of Healthcare Provider and Systems (CAHPS) surveys, a peer survey for physicians who provide consultation services, and a multi-source feedback survey focused on teamwork. All four of these new modules reflect the growing importance of the competencies of professionalism, communication, interpersonal skills, quality improvement, and safety in providing high-quality, patient-centered care.

One of the core strengths of these modules is that the more detailed, specific data enable physicians to make more specific and meaningful changes in their practice as part of their quality improvement. Given that most of these types of assessment surveys are best used for formative purposes, providing meaningful, actionable feedback is essential to their utility in helping physicians improve. As more health systems look to create patient-centered care programs and environments, actionable input from patients will be essential.

In other pioneering work, ABIM researchers found that trainees who receive lower ratings of competence in professionalism are
more likely to experience adverse licensing actions from state medical boards, underscoring the critical need for institutions involved
in graduate medical education to both model and assess professionalism as a core competency (Papadakis et al., 2008). This work has
added further support to the importance of assessing professionalism early in training as well as in practice.

The ABIM, along with others, has also recognized and studied
the importance of institutional culture and systems for promoting effective professionalism. Pioneering work by Hafferty found
that the "hidden curriculum" of academic institutions, referring to
what trainees actually experienced and what they see role-modeled
by more senior physicians, is far more powerful than any formal
curriculum of teaching about professionalism (Hafferty, 1998).
Further work examined the "avowed" versus "disavowed" values
of professionals and institutions. For example, an institution may
teach and endorse the importance of reducing the overuse of procedures, an "avowed professional value," yet support behaviors that
lead to overuse for economic gain (the "disavowed professional
value") (Ginsburg et al., 2003). This work, among others, high-
lights the powerful influence of culture and systems on individual
professional behaviors. The future of assessment of professionalism
will need to incorporate the effects of institutional and system values into the process, the next step in the evolution in competency
measurement.

CONCLUSION

Specialty boards such as the ABIM play an important role in promoting professionalism. The extent to which all boards promote

professionalism as accountability through assessment has grown, and in the case of ABIM has been bolstered by a commitment to rigor that has provided important leadership. Furthermore, ABIM and the ABIM Foundation have expanded their impact on professionalism beyond assessment, into advocacy, scholarship, and collaboration, yielding a result that serves as a model for the potential impact that can be achieved through a coordinated, multifaceted effort.

References

ABIM Foundation, American Board of Internal Medicine, American College of Physicians–American Society of Internal Medicine. Medical professionalism in the new millennium: a physician charter. *Ann Intern Med.* 2002;136(3):243–246.

AMSA Scorecard. Available at http://www.amsascorecard.org/executive-summary, accessed July 20, 2012.

Blank LL. Assessment of candidates' ethics and humanistic values. In: Mancall E, Bashook P, Dockery JL, eds. *Establishing Standards for Board Certification.* Evanston, IL: American Board of Medical Specialties; 1994:27–38.

Bodenheimer T. Coordinating care—a perilous journey through the health care system. *NEJM.* 2008;358:1064–1071.

Brennan T, Rothman D, Blank L, et al. Health industry practices that create conflicts of interest. *JAMA.* 2006;295:429–443.

Cassel CK, Guest J. Choosing wisely: helping physicians and patients make smart decisions about their care. *JAMA.* 2012. Published online April 4, 2012. doi:10.1001/jama.2012.476

Cassel, CK, Jain SH. Assessing individual physician performance: does measurement suppress motivation? *JAMA.* 2012;307(24):2595–2596

Ginsburg S, Regehr G, Lingard L. The disavowed curriculum. *J Gen Intern Med.* 2003;18:1015–1022.

Guide to Awareness and Evaluation of Humanistic Qualities. 2nd ed. Philadelphia: American Board of Internal Medicine; 1992–1995.

Hafferty FW. Beyond curriculum reform: confronting medicine's hidden curriculum. *Acad Med.* 1998;73:403–407.

Hall W, Violato C, Lewkonia R. Assessment of physician performance in Alberta: the Physician Achievement Review Project. *CMAJ.* 1999;161:52–57.

Lesser CS, Lucey C, Egener B, Braddock CH, Linas SL, Levinson W. A behavioral and systems view of professionalism. *JAMA.* 2010;304(24):2732–2737.

Lipner RS, Blank LL, Leas BF, Fortna GS. The value of patient and peer ratings in recertification. *Acad Med*. 2002;77(10 suppl):S64–S66.

Papadakis MA, Arnold GK, Blank LL, Holmboe ES, Lipner RS. Performance during internal medicine residency training and subsequent disciplinary action by state licensing boards. *Ann Intern Med*. 2008;148:869–876.

Ramsey PG, Wenrich MD, Carline JD. Use of peer ratings to evaluate physician performance. *JAMA*. 1993;269:1655–1660.

Wenrich MD, Carline JD, Giles LM, Ramsey PG. Ratings of the performances of practicing internists by hospital-based registered nurses. *Acad Med*. 1993;68:680–687.

Chapter 5

Medical Professionalism in the Twenty-First Century

CATHERINE D. DEANGELIS

Although the exact meaning of professionalism is open to debate, the Hippocratic Oath is arguably the earliest description of how physicians are to behave; or, to put it another way, what medical professionalism was, at least at that time (i.e., the sixth or fifth century B.C.). Ever since the published definition of the word *professionalism* by *Webster's Dictionary* in 1856, defining exactly what the term means for physicians and others involved in patient care has generated numerous discussions and publications over time (Medical Professionalism, 2002; Doctors in Society, 2005). That is understandable, as the term has taken on different meanings in various times, and this seems to be especially true for the twenty-first century. Attempting to find a workable definition using the Internet in these modern times nets little of value. For example, *Merriman-Webster's Dictionary* currently defines *professionalism* as "the conduct, aims, or qualities that characterize or mark a profession or a professional person." So, exactly what is the conduct and what are the aims and qualities that currently define medical professionalism?

However medical professional behavior is defined, one basic characteristic involves considering the practice of medicine a vocation, not a job. The primary professional responsibility of a physician is to protect and advocate for the patient. Furthermore, whatever else medical professional behavior might entail, arrogance is definitely not included. *Webster's* defines *arrogance* as "an attitude of superiority manifested in an overbearing manner or in presumptuous claims or assumptions." Unfortunately, some physicians manifest such behavior with patients and with their colleagues. Since a team effort, including physicians, nurses, public health officials, dentists, pharmacists, social workers, and other health care associates, is essential to assure good patient care, arrogance is the antithesis of professionalism. Additionally, physicians' arrogance in refusing to acknowledge suggestions from others with expertise to contribute to the care of patients for whom they have primary responsibility can harm patients. Examples are discouraging patients from seeking second opinions, or not including other members of the health care team in decisions when appropriate.

Medical professionalism might involve having some of the qualities of a "hero," but a physician need not be a hero to practice medical professionalism. According to *Wikipedia*, the word *hero*, coined in English in 1387, derives from the Greek word for *protector* or *defender* and defines a hero as someone who in the face of danger, adversity, or weakness displays self-sacrifice for some greater good. Physicians display such characteristics when they protect patients from harm, rather than enhancing their own self-interest. Examples include the obvious: caring for patients who have very communicable, serious diseases or caring for soldiers in battle; and less obviously, when physicians refuse to use more expensive or possibly more dangerous medications despite insistent patients who have been enchanted by direct-to-consumer advertisements, or when physicians refuse to order unnecessary (usually expensive) tests despite encouragement by business managers to do so, or refuse to perform unnecessary procedures despite fears of an unwarranted malpractice suit. This aspect of professionalism is also involved when a physician investigator refuses to put the name of someone, including his or her own, on a publication when it would be dishonest to do so, despite knowing that the person requesting that he or she do so might harm the physician's career. Whether or not "heroic," these examples are in the spirit of the best of the profession and are essential to protecting medical professionalism.

Traditionally, the medical profession has been characterized by six characteristics: a code of ethics, advanced knowledge and skills, regulation of education and professional conduct, high standards, substantial rewards, and autonomy—all of which were based on a responsibility for patient care in which trust was the foundation. While all these characteristics remain true to a degree, many of them are now manifested differently. A more modern characterization might be as shown in Figure 5.1 below, noting that the hub of medical professionalism is trust: trust manifested by patients, colleagues, and society in general.

Special knowledge and skills, as based on education and training, remains important in modern times, but to a far more advanced degree because of the enormous advances of medical science, technology, and the Internet. That special knowledge and those skills depend

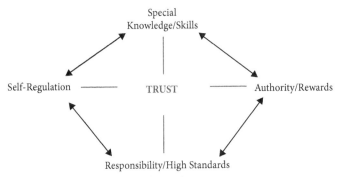

Figure 5.1 Components of medical professionalism.

on formal classroom teaching and clinical education and training as formulated by set standards and requirements. Maintenance of specialized knowledge and skills is also essential to assure good patient care (ABMS Maintenance of Certification, 2012).

Teaching involving specialized knowledge and skills begins with the medical school curriculum in classroom and clinical settings and extends throughout the lifetime of a physician. The formal curriculum aspects of this teaching are usually well organized and controlled by the dean's office in keeping with guidelines from the Licensing Council on Medical Education (LCME). Teaching professionalism as part of the formal classroom-based curriculum is only one (and possibly a relatively small) part of how physicians acquire such knowledge. More important is what medical students and young residents observe and feel in everyday encounters with older, more experienced physicians, the so-called hidden curriculum. These encounters can involve situations in which medical students are exposed to the unprofessional treatment of patients, colleagues, and themselves. In some situations, the student might be treated unprofessionally by verbal and physical abuse and sexual harassment (Silver and Glicken, 1990). This unprofessional behavior towards others by physicians is often a display of unwarranted power and arrogance and can have a profound effect on students and young faculty and their ultimate behavior with others.

A very important but often neglected part of imparting knowledge is mentoring, which is an important aspect of academic and continuing education contributing to the mentee's personal development, career development, choice of specialty, research productivity (including grant support), and publications. Academic medical centers and individuals who support mentoring enhance talent-development, leadership capacity, and institutional stability. However, in one study (Sambujak et al., 2006), less than 50% of medical students and, in some specialties, less than 20% of faculty reported having a mentor. In addition, women's perceptions were that they had more difficulty than men in finding mentors. In another paper (Bickel and Rosenthal, 2011), the authors discuss how differences in sex, language, generation, and ethnicity interfere with mentoring relationships.

A review of PubMed literature from 2000 to 2008 revealed only 25 articles that met the authors' criteria for structured mentoring programs and surveys of medical students' mentoring. In these programs, the personal faculty–student mentoring helped students with career choices, increased their research productivity, and improved their general medical school performance; and the medical students reported a higher overall sense of well-being (Frei et al., 2010). So, are there only 25 articles because there are so few structured mentoring programs, or merely because the many other such programs have not been reported? We can only hope the latter is true.

Authority and rewards emanate from patients' seeking care from physicians whom patients believe to have the knowledge and skills necessary to help them. With these come high social status and substantial financial rewards. Of course, this authority and these rewards must be earned by providing good care, noting that this takes continued acquisition of knowledge requiring the physician to keep up with the rapid and profound expansion of medical science and technology, and ultimately, requires concern for the patient. Good care also means really caring, in a social and vocational sense. Good care is not only assured by how smart or physically skilled a physician might be, but also by how much he or she really is concerned for and about the patient. This includes paying attention to the patient's story and providing for the patient's needs, including physical, psychological, and "spiritual" (Cobb, Puchalski, and Rumbold, 2012), and doing so with compassion. This requires a team approach, since essentially no single physician or other health professional can meet all these needs.

The demand for physician responsibility and high standards for assuring the best care and safety of patients in clinical practice, education, and research is stronger than ever, especially since the publication of the landmark Institute of Medicine report *To Err Is Human* (Kohn et al., 1999; Wachter, 2010). However, because of some serious lapses—including conflicts of interest and manipulation of education and research by for-profit companies, often with the cooperation of physicians—a high level of concern from the public has been generated.

Merriam-Webster's Collegiate Dictionary defines a *conflict of interest* (COI) as a "conflict between the private interests and the official responsibilities of a person in a position of trust." Clearly, a physician is in a position of trust. COIs may be perceived or real, potential or actual, inconsequential or harmful. Because of the very nature of human beings, COIs are inevitable and ubiquitous. However, those that can harm patients denigrate the physician and the medical profession. COIs can involve payment or other remuneration, affiliation, or consultancies that might result in harming patients. They involve clinicians who accept gifts such as dinners; tickets to sports or other events; registration and travel or other fees for attending meetings or conventions, when these gifts involve the use or promotion of drugs or medical devices that might be more expensive, more harmful, or otherwise not necessary for patients. To believe that such gifts or even lesser ones such as pens do not affect the use of specific drugs or devices is, at best, naïve. Why else would companies spend so much on such "gifts"?

Conflicts of interest also include the behavior of physicians who serve on speakers' bureaus for pharmaceutical or medical device for-profit companies in which these physicians use the company-prepared PowerPoint presentations that slant information to promote the company's drugs; or physicians who encourage off-label use of such drugs or devices; i.e., uses not approved by the Food and Drug Administration. These activities can result in harming patients, and they also denigrate the involved physicians and the medical profession.

COIs also involve investigators who allow the use of their names on published studies in which the investigator played no role, or investigators who allow manipulation of data or analysis to make a drug look more beneficial than it is (Ross et al., 2008; Bombardier et al., 2000). Also included are reviewers who do not recuse themselves from reviewing manuscripts covering areas in which they have a personal interest, or editors who allow such practices in order to increase the financial profitability of their journal or the journal's "impact factor" (IF). In fact "the IF," as currently used, has caused as much trouble as it has helped to define scientific quality. The IF that should matter, at least as much as the Impact Factor, is the Integrity Factor of a journal. Unfortunately, unlike the impact factor, the integrity factor measurement is not available, supposedly because integrity cannot be measured—much like caring, I suppose.

Recent literature on COIs has focused primarily on industry–investigator relationships, ethical considerations, and the undue influence of industry on clinicians who prescribe medications. According to PubMed, the number of annual articles published on COI have increased from a scant few from 1975 to the late 1980s, to a rapid rise from under 100 in the early 1990s, to 600 from 2005 to 2012. Of interest is that this annual increase began about the time that industry decided to marry their science divisions with their marketing divisions (Applebaum, 2009). This increased emphasis on marketing and decreased emphasis on scientific discovery by for-profit medical companies has resulted in having few drugs in the pipeline that could help patients (Government Accountability Office, 2006). In addition, an increased awareness and concern regarding physicians' COIs has led to public skepticism and has greatly harmed the medical profession.

Self-regulation (autonomy): Because the word *autonomy* has often been misunderstood to mean an arrogant freedom from outside regulation or oversight, the term *self-regulation* better describes the medical profession's concept of oversight and regulation by peers; that is, those with the same or equivalent, pertinent education, knowledge, and experience. Clearly, formal laws regulate how physicians practice in many ways, including licensure, scope of practice, standards of care, and liability. However, physician oversight of medical education regulation, specialty boards, and medical licensure boards, often with lay members serving on those committees and boards, forms the general foundation of self-regulation.

Unfortunately, at least one area dealing with peer oversight currently is not at a level that assures public trust. For example, it is rare for a physician to report a colleague whose practice is not at a reasonable level of expertise, or to sanction a colleague who accepts financial or other rewards for clinical practice or research that are not warranted.

Also harmful is allowing physician colleagues to ignore or denigrate other members of the health care team, even including maintenance workers. Imagine what professional life would be like without those who maintain a facility's physical appearance, cleanliness, delivery of supplies, transportation of patients, etc. These individuals are important for good patient care and should be acknowledged for their work.

Another aspect of self-regulation is physicians' assuring their own physical and psychological health. Working too many hours or in a continually stressful environment without taking time to rest and replenish their bodies and minds is harmful to themselves and ultimately to patients. There is no nobility in neglecting or denigrating your body or mind.

Self-regulation or autonomy depends on physicians' receiving sound education and training as overseen by governing bodies such as the Licensing Council on Medical Education (LCME) for medical students (accreditation of medical schools); the Accreditation Council on Graduate Medical Education (ACGME) for residents (accreditation of specialty training programs); the American Board of Medical Specialties (ABMS) for fellows (certification and maintenance of certification); the Accreditation Council on Continuing Medical Education (ACCME) for continuing education (accreditation of CME programs); and the various state medical licensing boards for the legal practice of medicine.

A significant problem that has arisen is litigation involving the medical profession. Under the medical malpractice law, a physician who fails to perform according to the medical profession's customary standard of care, resulting in injury of the patient, can be sued for negligence. When this occurs, the patient is entitled to compensation under the medical malpractice tort law, which is a set of rules governing injuries where crime or contract is not involved. It is absolutely essential that patients receive fair compensation for injuries resulting from the malpractice of physicians. However, in many cases, the very fear of malpractice has led physicians to order unnecessary tests and to perform unnecessary procedures resulting in great financial and emotional cost to patients, other physicians, and society. In these cases, physicians ignore what they believe to be good medical practice and that may very well actually be good medical practice because they fear a malpractice suit.

Is this fear of malpractice lawsuits warranted, especially since ordering unnecessary tests and procedures add substantially to the patient's angst and health care costs in the United States? According to one study, in 2009 there were 10,739 malpractice claims paid on behalf of physicians; 4910 (47.6%) involved inpatient settings; 4448 (43.1%) involved outpatient settings; and 966 (9.4%) involved both (Bishop et al., 2011). To put this in perspective, that same year there were 36.1 million hospitalizations (Hospitalizations, 2012) and 1.1 3 billion outpatient and physicians' office visits (Outpatient visits, 2012; Physicians' office visits, 2012).

Investigators in another study reviewed 1452 closed malpractice claims from five liability insurers to determine whether a medical injury had occurred and whether it resulted from a medical error. No verifiable medical injuries occurred in 3% of these cases, and 37% did not involve medical errors. Most of these cases (72% with no errors and 84% with no injuries) did not result in compensation. Of interest is that the overhead costs of malpractice litigation were "exorbitant," according to the authors (Studdert, 2006). Psychological costs to patients and to physicians were not investigated, but they must have been significant.

According to a 2009 Congressional Budget Office report, the total cost resulting from malpractice liability—including malpractice insurance settlements, out-of-court settlement awards, and administrative cost—was $35 billion in 2009, representing 2% of total United States health care expenditures (Malpractice Liability costs, 2012)

PRIMUM NON NOCERE

I used to wonder why *primum non nocere*, "first, do no harm," rather than "first, do good," was the basic tenet of medicine. After many years as a clinician, educator, researcher, administrator, and editor, I realize the wisdom of this doctrine. Doing good is wonderful and can be accomplished on a daily basis simply by providing the best care possible for patients, directly in clinical settings or indirectly in educational and research settings. Defining *best care* is where "do no harm" becomes so important. For example, keeping someone alive with drugs and machines when the likelihood of the patient's return to a reasonable life is highly unlikely is probably not doing good, and might be doing a great deal of harm to the patient and to his or her family. Ordering tests with a one in 100,000 or so likelihood of revealing a health problem might be considered good by some because there would be virtually no chance that the problem would be missed. However, the cost financially to patients and society and the unnecessary worry of patients and family members caused by a false positive result is harmful. This would be a reasonable opportunity for physicians to assume their civic duty as part of a social contract to lead a real initiative disclosing, with sound data and while assuring the compensation of patients injured by malpractice, the wisdom of allowing bureaucratic decisions to trump medical knowledge. After all, protecting patients is at the very heart of medical professionalism.

Medical investigators, authors, reviewers, and editors have a special requirement to do no harm because their work can involve many patients beyond those for whom they provide direct care. Published articles are read by many who care directly for patients or who educate physicians who care or will care for patients, hence the greater responsibility. The recent incredible rise in publication retractions (Steen, 2010) reveals how great harm can be done by publishing papers that affect patient care and are based on false or manipulated data.

COMMODIFICATION OF THE MEDICAL PROFESSION

According to Wikipedia, "Commodification, which describes assignment of economic value to something not previously considered in economic terms, is sometimes used to describe the transformation of the market for a unique, branded product into a market based on undifferentiated products." Furthermore, according to *Wikipedia*, "commodification (or commoditization) is the transformation of goods, ideas, or other entities that may not normally be regarded as goods as a commodity." Stated simply, commodification is the assignment of an economic value to an entity not usually or previously considered in economic terms. In other words, the entity becomes something that can be bought and sold.

According to Uwe Reinhardt (personal communication), economists generally are guided by the adage that the value of something is what it can be sold for. So, by commodification of the medical profession, if a physician is considered in that term, he or she becomes a commodity rather than a professional. Economists and business persons believe that almost everything can be marketed (that is, sold), even names on buildings, laboratories, rooms, baseballs, etc., so why not the medical profession? Of course, physicians provide a service for which they should be appropriately reimbursed, but if that is the primary reason physicians care for patients, the true meaning of the medical profession is lost, and economists proven correct. Certainly the vast majority of physicians do not think this way, and it is a rare medical student who enters medical school with this attitude. However, there has been a gradual encroachment of the bureaucratic business model into medical practice, with business managers inserting themselves into decisions that should be the sole realm of physicians, such as what tests or drugs should be ordered or treatments rendered.

According to a 2005 National Academy of Sciences report, ordering unnecessary tests or treatments might account for up to 30% of health care costs in the United States (Reid et al., 2005). In 2010, total health care expenditures accounted for 17.9% of the gross domestic product in the United States, which was 5% more than the next-ranked country, the Netherlands (World Bank, 210). No matter what the public might think about the quality of health care in the United States, the consensus is that it costs too much. Clearly, one way physicians can curtail some costs is to stop ordering unnecessary tests and performing unnecessary treatments as dictated by the business model rather than by the medical professional model.

Another way bureaucracy has infiltrated the medical profession in an attempt to commodify physicians is by language. There is no term used for physicians that causes me more consternation than *provider.* Closely behind in generating consternation is using the term *consumer* or *client* for "patient." Certainly physicians provide care to patients, but clumping physicians together with all health-related individuals (and even institutions in some cases) as *providers* is confusing at best, and possibly demeaning at worst. *Wikipedia* includes physicians in the definition of *provider* as "...an individual health care provider (also known as a health worker)...." Health workers include individuals with a broad spectrum of education, knowledge, experience, and responsibility. Clearly there is a big difference between, for example, a health aide and a physician. So why not differentiate by using the term *physician* or *clinician* (including physicians, nurses, dentists, and physician assistants) when referring to these individuals? Why not, indeed!

Where did the custom of calling physicians "providers" originate? The best resource I could find to answer this question is an article by William Safire, in which he states that the earliest citation to this use he could find was in a *New York Times* article published on February 24, 1972, about New York City's Medicaid program. The term "provider" is attributed to Julie M. Sugarman, then the New York Administrator of Human Resources. According to Safire, Sugarman attributed the term to Title 19 of the Social Security Act passed in 1965. However, Safire could not find that term in the Act, so who knows where it originated (Safire, 1993).

No matter the origin of the terms *provider* for *physicians* or *consumer/client* for *patients*: it's not very difficult to understand that using "physician" interchangeably with "provider," or "patient" with "consumer/client," allows business persons, bureaucrats, and others to have control over physicians that might well not be possible otherwise. For example, the public seems to have little concern when a "provider" is told that he or she can only spend six minutes with a consumer/client, but they probably would take umbrage if they knew their physician could be so limited by business managers in the case of patients. Furthermore, can you imagine a mother proudly introducing "…my son, the provider"? Clearly it works neither as a joke nor as a characterization, and it certainly does not do justice to physicians. So why don't all physicians refuse to use or even acknowledge that term when referring to physicians? Good question.

CONCLUSION

Much of what I've written is, or should be, obvious. However, to paraphrase George Orwell, stating the obvious is the duty of intelligent persons. We all need to be reminded of why we became and remain members of the medical profession and what that requires of us all.

References

ABMS Maintenance of Certification. Available at www.abms.org/maintenamce_of_certification/ABMS_MOC.aspx. http://www.abms.org/maintenance_of_certification/Accessed MARCH 25, 2013
Applebaum K. Is marketing the enemy of pharmaceutical innovation? *Hastings Cent Rep.* 2009;39(4):13–17.

Bickel J, Rosenthal SL. Difficult issues in mentoring: recommendations on making the "undiscussable" discussable. *Acad Med.* 2011;86:1229–1234.

Bishop TF, Ryan AM, Casalino LP. Paid malpractice claims for adverse events in inpatient and outpatient settings. *JAMA.* 2011; 305:2427–2431.

Bombardier C, Laine L, Reicin A, et al. Comparison of upper gastrointestinal toxicity of rofecoxib and naproxen in patients with rheumatoid arthritis. *N Engl J Med.* 2000;343:1520–1528.

Cobb M, Puchalski CM, Rumbold B. *Spirituality in Health Care.* New York: Oxford University Press; 2012.

Doctors in Society. *Medical Professionalism in a Changing World. Report of a Working Party.* London: Royal College of Physicians; 2005.

Frei E, Stamm M, Buddeberg-Fischer B. Mentoring programs for medical students—a review of the PubMed literature, 2000–2008. *BMC Med Educ.* 2010;10:32.

Government Accountability Office. New drug development: science, business, regulatory, and intellectual property issues cited as hampering drug development efforts. 2006. Available at http//www.gao.gov/new.items/do749.pdf. Accessed September 18, 2012.

Hospitalizations in the U.S. Available at http://www.cdc.gov/nchs/fastats/hospital.htm Accessed July 29, 2012.

Kohn LT, Corigan JM, Donaldson MS, eds. *To Err Is Human: Building a Safer Health System.* Washington DC: National Academy Press; 1999.

Malpractice liability. Available at www.cbo.gov/sites/default/files/cbo files/ftpdocs/106 xx/doc 10641/10 – 09 – tort reform.Pdf.

Medical professionalism in the new millennium: a physician charter. *Ann Int Med.* 2002;136(3):243–246.

Outpatient visits. Available at www.cdc.gov/nchs/fastats/docvisit.htm. Accessed March 25, 2013.

Physicians' office visits. Available at http://www.cdc.gov/nchs/fastats/docvisit.htm. Accessed March 25, 2013.

Reid PP, Compton WD, Grossman JH and Fanjiang G, eds. *Building a Better Delivery System.* Washington, DC: National Academy Press; 2005.

Ross JS, Hill, KP, Egilman DS, Krumholz HM. Guest authorship and ghostwriting in publications related to rofecoxib: a case study of industry documents from rofecoxib litigation. *JAMA.* 2008;299:1739–1756.

Safire W. On Language: Health care provider, heal thyself. New York Times, April 11, 1993.

Sambujak D, Straus SE, Marusic A. Mentoring in academic medicine: a systematic review. *JAMA.* 2006;296:1103–1115.

Silver HK, Glicken AD. Medical student abuse: incidence, severity and significance. *JAMA.* 1990;263:527–532.

Steen RG. Retractions in the scientific literature: do authors deliberately commit research fraud? *J Med Ethics*, 2011;37:113–117.

Studdert DM, Mello MM, Gawande AA, et al. Claims, errors, and compensation payments in medical malpractice litigation. *N Engl J Med*. 2006;354: 2024–2033.

Wachter RM. Patient safety at 10: Unmistakable progress, troubling gaps. *Health Aff. (Millwood)*. 2010;29:165–173.

World Bank. Health care expenditures. Available at http://data.worldbank.org/indicator/SH.XPD.TOTL.ZS Accessed November 30, 2012.

Chapter 6

Professionalism and Nursing—
A Quest or an Accomplishment?

KATHLEEN M. WHITE

The nursing profession is the largest segment of the health care workforce, with almost 3 million registered nurses in the United States and over 12 million nurses worldwide. Nurses practice in many settings, including hospitals, outpatient and ambulatory clinics, long-term care facilities, schools, homes, occupational health clinics, community centers, ambulatory surgery centers, urgent care facilities, retail clinics, and physicians' offices. Nurses contribute to health care through many different roles and specialties, and discussions about future roles for nursing are endless. Nursing has been rated as the most trusted profession in all but one year of a CNN/*USA Today*/Gallup poll that has asked the public to rate the honesty and ethical standards of 23 different professions. So, why does nursing struggle with defining itself as a profession? How important is professionalism for nurses? Today's health care environment demands a team of professionals, including nurses, working together to provide care for patients and appreciating the contributions of each professional member of the team. Public debate and the literature have seen a long struggle to define professionalism for nursing.

HISTORY OF NURSING PROFESSIONALISM

This abbreviated discussion of nursing history is intended to focus on events in nursing's history that specifically relate to the development of nursing professionalism. The birth of modern nursing took place mainly in religious orders. Nursing developed as a female-dominated occupation from Victorian times, and societal values placed this female-dominated nursing discipline subservient to the male-dominated medical profession (Turkoski, 1995).

In 1860, Florence Nightingale laid the foundation for professional nursing with the establishment of the first secular nursing school in the world at St. Thomas' Hospital in London. She viewed nursing as an art as well as a science requiring a dedicated curriculum of study. *Notes on Nursing* (Nightingale, 1860) served as the cornerstone for the development of early nursing curricula. Nightingale's experience and early generation of nursing knowledge caused her to advocate for sanitary living conditions as of great importance to reducing deaths among soldiers, and later, her advocacy for the sanitary design of hospitals. She also attempted to raise the standard for potential nursing students, attempting to improve nursing as an acceptable form of female participation in the workforce.

The first training schools for nurses were managed by physicians and associated with hospitals founded and led by those physicians (Kalisch and Kalisch, 1995). In the latter part of the nineteenth century, as modern medicine made scientific strides and hospital use increased, some of the "art" of medicine found its way into the nursing domain, and nurses found themselves involved in more complicated treatment of patients (Kalisch and Kalisch, 1995). As hospitals proliferated, so did nursing schools, in order to develop a means to provide nursing care in those hospitals. Simultaneously, and for decades into the twentieth century, a heated debate raged over the education provided in these training schools and whether nurses should even be educated in both theory and practice, limiting the development of nursing knowledge and restricting the quest for nursing professionalism.

In 1893, the superintendent of the Farrand Training School for Nurses in Detroit, Michigan, insisted that nurses needed a code of ethics to guide their work. Consequently, the "Florence Nightingale Pledge" was developed, similar to the medical profession's Hippocratic Oath:

I solemnly pledge myself before God and in the presence of this assembly to pass my life in purity and to practice my profession faithfully.

I will abstain from whatever is deleterious and mischievous and will not take or knowingly administer any harmful drug.

I will do all in my power to maintain and elevate the standard of my profession and will hold in confidence all personal matters committed to my keeping and all family affairs coming to my knowledge in the practice of my calling.

With loyalty will I endeavor to aid the physician in his work and devote myself to the welfare of those committed to my care.

(Deans and Austin, 1936, p58.)

Nursing students still recite this pledge at pinning and graduation ceremonies today.

The American Society of Superintendents of Training Schools of Nursing (ASSTSN), the first national nursing organization, met in 1894 to promote fellowship of its members, establish universal standards for training nurses, and further the interests of the nursing profession. Four years later, the Nurses Associated Alumnae of the United States and Canada was officially established as the first professional organization for nurses (Kalisch and Kalisch, 1995). In

1911, the name was changed to the American Nurses Association to incorporate other nursing societies, in addition to educators (American Nurses Association, 1996).

In 1922, the Rockefeller Foundation appointed Josephine Goldmark to lead a committee for the study of nursing education. The Goldmark report (1923) emphasized the need to establish university schools of nursing, and identified a lack of money dedicated for nursing education as a barrier to implementing higher standards of education for nurses. Within five years, 25 colleges developed programs in association with hospital nursing schools. Yale University became the first autonomous university school of nursing in 1924, followed by Case Western Reserve University and Vanderbilt University. However, there was not a large movement to develop these university nursing schools (Kalisch and Kalisch, 1995).

Another effort to upgrade the discipline of nursing followed, in the formal creation of the Army and Navy Nurse Corps after World War I. The authorizing legislation required the Superintendent of the Army Nurse Corps to be a hospital nursing school graduate and nurses in the corps to be graduates of a nursing school. This was an important step in the professionalization of nursing, raising the status of this new corps above the "Hospital Corps" that previously included both formally trained and untrained nurses (Kalisch and Kalisch, 1995).

In 1946, the American Nurses Association (ANA), in collaboration with the National League for Nursing Education and the National Organization for Public Health Nursing, met to confront the declining working conditions for the nation's nurses. They developed a 10-point platform of reform that included a statement endorsing the state and district nursing associations as qualified to provide for the economic security of nurses and represent them through collective bargaining, countering growing union organization for nurses (Kalisch and Kalisch, 1995; ANA, 1996). Although the ANA's assembly unanimously adopted the national economic security program that included collective bargaining, controversy over the right of nurses to engage in collective bargaining raged for decades and has been central to the debate about nursing professionalism (ANA, 1996). Central to this debate is whether nursing is a calling or just a job or trade (Turkoski, 1995).

This very important convention also raised the question of who should pay for nursing education (Polifko, 2011). It was generally agreed that nursing education should be paid for by the individual student, the student's family, or through grants, loans, or scholarships, and not be provided free of charge by the hospital where the training takes place, in exchange for long and difficult work assignments. Prior to this time, obstacles to nursing reform came from hospital and medical societies determined to maintain the servitude status of nursing students and limit opportunities for nursing graduates. Following World War II, because of nursing shortages and the declining interest in nursing as a career choice, an anti–university education sentiment arose among nurses questioning the need for this higher level of education. Those concerned nurses wondered who would provide bedside nursing care if most nurses were to be educated as supervisors and educators. This dealt another blow to the movement toward nursing professionalism, this time from within profession.

In 1948, the Russell Sage Foundation released the "Brown report," entitled *Nursing for the Future* (Brown, 1948). Once again, a report detailed the problems with nursing education, and its central importance to advancing the professionalism of nursing. The report recommended the development of standards for accreditation of nursing schools; that an accreditation and re-accreditation process be put in place immediately; and that a nationwide educational campaign be conducted to rally broad public support for accredited schools and for identifying non-accredited schools (Brown, 1948).

The national nursing organizations began to develop an accreditation process for nursing schools through the establishment of the Committee to Implement the Brown Report. The Committee started with an assessment of criteria previously developed by the professional organizations and used by nursing schools. It classified the schools into three groups or ranks, of which only 25% met the criteria for the highest classification. After this first assessment of nursing schools, the National League for Nursing began to develop nursing educational standards and help schools understand how to meet them.

Because of a critical national nursing shortage after World War II, the first associate degree nursing education program was established at Teacher's College at Columbia University in 1952 to produce more nurses faster and move nursing education firmly into higher education and away from hospital schools of nursing. However, this attempt to raise the standards of nursing education created another pathway into the profession. Despite all its good intentions, the discipline's quest for professionalism was once again dealt a setback that is still an issue for the nursing profession today.

In 1956, the federal government's Professional Nurse Traineeship Program, an important source of money for nursing education, renewed federal aid to nurses previously allocated during World War II. These Title II funds authorized money to registered nurses (RNs) to study administration, supervision, and education. In 1964, Title VIII was added to the Public Health Service Act specifically for nursing education. The funds provided money to build nursing schools, expand nursing programs, reimburse diploma nursing programs for student education costs, continue the professional traineeship program, and provide long-term, low-interest loans for students to attend nursing school (U.S. Public Health Service, 1997). The 1975 Nurse Training Act continued the previous provisions and added a separate authorization for advanced nursing education. Because of this legislation, the 1970s and 1980s saw a big upswing in the numbers of nurses who pursued graduate degrees in nursing. These graduate degrees in nursing focused on specialization in a clinical area as well as preparation in a role such as administration, education, research, nurse practitioner, or clinical nurse specialist.

The final development toward professionalism in nursing's history was the quest to generate nursing knowledge. Most early research in nursing focused on education and not on the work of the profession. The ANA launched a nursing research program in 1950 to study characteristics of nurses, employment settings and relationships, changing the focus from research on nursing education to the work of nursing in an attempt to define and measure the work and the difference that nursing interventions make for quality health care. They formalized this program of nursing research in 1955 through the establishment of the American Nurses Foundation (ANA, 1996).

At the same time, federal support for nursing research began within the U.S. Public Health Service's Division of Nursing through an extramural nursing research program in its Research Grants and Fellowship Branch (United States Public Health Service, 1997). Additionally, the National Institutes of Health (NIH) also established the Nursing Research Study Section in its Division of Research Grants to review the growing number of nursing research applications. However, it took another 30 years until an Institute of Medicine report recommended that nursing research be included in the mainstream of biomedical and behavioral research. In 1985, the Center for Nursing Research within the NIH was created out of Public Law 99-158, and in 1993, the Center was elevated to Institute status. The National Institute of Nursing Research was created in the NIH, putting nursing research on par with research in the other health care professions (USPHS, 1997).

Throughout the twentieth century, nurses' opinions were divided about the role the discipline should play in women's movement, beginning first with suffrage for women through the long journey for women's rights. Many felt that nurses should focus only on matters of health care and not politics. The political-advocacy role of the ANA did not flourish until the 1970s with its endorsement of the Equal Rights Amendment (Turkoski, 1995). Liberal and socialist feminist theory discusses the problems with the male-dominated institution of professionalism for a predominately female discipline (Wuest, 1994).

THE DEVELOPMENT OF NURSING AS A PROFESSION

In order to understand the concept of professionalism, we need to define the word *profession* and consider how nursing meets the definition. Professions are defined by generally accepted criteria that distinguish the professions from other occupations. In some of the earliest work defining professions, Wilensky noted that occupations pass through a rather consistent sequence of stages on their way to becoming "professions":

(1) creation of a full-time occupation;

(2) establishment of a training school that reflects both the knowledge base of a profession and the efforts to improve the lot of the occupation;

(3) formation of a professional association for the occupation to define the nature of the professional tasks of the occupation; and

(4) formation of a code of ethics for both the members of the occupation and for its clients and the public. (Wilensky, 1964)

The challenge to discussion of nursing professionalism is seen in the history of a discipline that has tried to follow a set of male-generated objective criteria for professionalism (Turkoski, 1995).

In 1968, Hall defined a set of key indicators for the nursing profession, to include:

(1) creation of a professional organization as a major source of ideas and decision making about the work of the profession;

(2) existence of a code of ethics and a belief that service to the public is a major component of the work of the profession;

(3) belief that the profession should engage in self-regulation for the work of the profession (a social contract with society for self-governance);

(4) sense of calling and status to the profession that is exhibited in dedication of the individual to the work of the profession;

(5) development of ongoing, systematic knowledge about the work of the profession;

(6) transfer of this knowledge through education; and

(7) autonomous decision making by professionals about the work of the profession without external pressures from clients, employers, or the public. (Flexner, 1910; Hall, 1968)

In describing a professional model for nursing, Hall also suggested that each profession needs to develop its own method of measuring professionalism. Hall's "Professionalism Inventory" identified five key indicators of an individual's attitude toward professionalism:

(1) use of a professional organization as the major source of ideas and judgments for the professional;

(2) belief that the profession was created to serve the public;

(3) belief that the profession must be self-regulating;
(4) belief in a sense of calling to the work of the profession (vocation); and
(5) belief in the importance of autonomy in decision making about the work. (Hall, 1968)

This tool has been used by many nurse researchers; and, interestingly, research has shown that there has been a shift in attitudes since 1968 when Hall designed the original tool (Wynd, 2003). Nurses are now more interested in autonomy and membership in professional organizations and less focused on belief in public service and sense of calling (Cary, 2001).

As the professional organization for nurses in the United States, the ANA defines the nursing's accountability and autonomy by virtue of its status as a profession. This information is disseminated to the profession and the public through three foundational publications that define nursing, set standards for the practice of nursing, and outline nursing's code of ethics (ANA, 2001; ANA 2010a; ANA 2010b). "Being professional" is the act of behaving in a manner defined and expected by the chosen profession. Nurses are accountable for their knowledge, skills, and behavior to self, institution, regulatory and legal entities, and their profession. They have autonomy to act independently and make appropriate decisions as they pertain to the control over their own practice. This autonomy and accountability for practice are governed by nursing's scope and standards of practice (White and O'Sullivan, 2012). In the late 1990s, the ANA, in collaboration with other nursing organizations, began a formal process for the recognition of nursing specialties. This process involves the recognition of the specialty, approval of a scope-of-practice statement for the nursing specialty, and acknowledgement of the specialty's standards of practice assuring autonomy and accountability for that nursing specialty practice (White and O'Sullivan, 2012).

WHAT DOES PROFESSIONALISM IN NURSING MEAN?

Hendelman (2009) defined the term *professionalism* as embracing a set of attitudes, skills, behaviors, attributes, and values that are expected from those to whom society has extended the privilege of being considered "a professional." The core values of professionalism include: honesty and integrity, altruism, respect, responsibility and accountability, compassion and empathy, dedication, and self-improvement.

Do these core values capture nursing professionalism? As Hall (1968) suggested, each profession must determine its own criteria for professionalism.

The ANA defines five tenets that determine the professional practice of nursing. They are that:

(1) Nursing practice is individualized to meet the unique needs of the patient, family, or situation;
(2) Nurses coordinate care by establishing relationships with patients, families, and communities, and through collaborative interprofessional teams;
(3) Caring is central to the practice of nursing, part of the everyday professionalism beyond compassion and empathy, which are often individually shown;
(4) Nurses use theory and evidence-based knowledge of human experiences and responses to plan, assess, diagnose; identify outcomes; plan, implement, and evaluate care; and
(5) A strong link exists between the professional work environment and the nurse's ability to provide quality care. (ANA, 2010a)

Additionally, through ANA collaborative work, Nursing's Professional Model for Regulation of Nursing Practice was developed to describe the profession's responsibility for self-regulation of nursing practice and the responsibility shared among the profession, the official regulatory agencies, and the individual nurse. The model serves as a guide to professional decision making for nursing practice (Styles et al., 2008). The base of the pyramid represents the professional and specialty nursing organization's responsibility to define the scope and standards of practice for nursing. The next level is the state's responsibility to develop regulation for licensing. The third level of the pyramid represents the institutions' obligation to define policies and procedures to provide additional regulation for nursing practice. The top level of the pyramid represents nursing's self-determination or professional autonomy for decision making after considering all other levels of regulation. (See Figure 6.1—Model of Professional Nursing Practice Regulation.) Nurses are expected

Figure 6.1 Model of Professional Nursing Practice Regulation

to engage in self-regulation and act in the best interests of the public at all times.

Standards reflect the values and priorities of the professional and provide the direction for professional practice, serve as a guide for evaluation of that practice, and define the profession's accountability to the public for their practice (White and O'Sullivan, 2012). The ANA Standards of Professional Performance address how the RN conducts herself or himself in practice and delineate the framework for which "registered nurses are accountable for their professional actions to themselves, their patients, their peers and ultimately society" (ANA, 2010, p. 11). The Professional Performance Standards address how the RN conducts herself or himself in practice, and are as follows:

Ethics: The registered nurse practices ethically.

Education: The registered nurse attains knowledge and competence that reflect current nursing practice.

Evidence-Based Practice and Research: The registered nurse integrates evidence and research findings into practice.

Quality of Practice: The registered nurse contributes to quality nursing practice.

Communication: The registered nurse communicates effectively in a variety of formats in all areas of practice.

Leadership: The registered nurse demonstrates leadership in the professional practice setting and the profession.

Collaboration: The registered nurse collaborates with healthcare consumer, family, and others in the conduct of nursing practice.

Professional Practice Evaluation: The registered nurse evaluates one's own nursing practice in relation to professional practice standards and guidelines, relevant statutes, rules, and regulations.

Resource Utilization: The registered nurse utilizes appropriate resources to plan and provide nursing services that are safe, effective, and financially responsible.

Environmental Health: The registered nurse practices in an environmentally safe and healthy manner.

ANA's position statement, "Professional Role Competence" (ANA, 2008) articulates the importance of competence for the nursing professional:

> *The public has a right to expect registered nurses to demonstrate professional competence throughout their careers. ANA believes the registered nurse is individually responsible and accountable for maintaining professional competence. The ANA further believes that it is the nursing profession's responsibility to shape and guide any process for assuring nurse competence. Regulatory agencies define minimal standards for regulation of practice to protect the public. The employer is responsible and accountable to provide an environment conducive to competent practice. Assurance of competence is the shared responsibility of the profession, individual nurses, professional organizations, credentialing and certification entities, regulatory agencies, employers, and other key stakeholders. (ANA, 2008)*

Other nursing professional organizations worldwide have developed similar standards of practice (Registered Nursing Association of Ontario [RNAO], 2007). The RNAO, a member of the CNA, identified eight attributes of professionalism that are similar in nature to the ANA's Professional Practice standards: knowledge, spirit of inquiry, accountability, autonomy, advocacy, innovator/visionary, collegiality/collaboration, and ethics/values.

CONTEMPORARY NURSING PROFESSIONALISM

While discussion continues in the literature as to the meaning of professionalism, the following two examples from the ANA and the CNA provide general agreement about the attributes of professionalism for nursing practice. Nurses apply these attributes daily in their practice, whether it entails clinical care, research, education, policy, or administration.

Knowledge is a key attribute of professionalism, enabling a profession like nursing to define the work of that profession. Professionalism in nursing requires that nurses be committed to the discovery and generation of new knowledge through research and the application of knowledge in their everyday work to maintain an evidence-based practice.

A strong educational system is another key attribute of professionalism. Nursing professionalism requires that nurses complete accredited nursing education programs and meet minimum criteria for licensure and/or certification. However, because health care is always changing and evolving, true professionalism is exhibited in every nurse's responsibility for continued competence through lifelong learning.

A third attribute of professionalism is autonomy in practice and decision making. The nursing profession enjoys an autonomous practice within their scope of practice, as defined by the professional organizational and state licensure agencies. Nurses are held accountable for using the nursing process as the problem-solving and decision making framework to guide their practice. Use of a systematic methodology, such as the nursing process, ensures a deliberate and consistent approach to nursing care. The professional is held accountable for this process as defined by the ANA's Standards of Nursing Practice (ANA, 2010). These standards, in addition to the Standards of Professional Performance described earlier, establish the legal standard of care and a nurse's duty as a professional. Rutledge (2011), in describing the autonomy and accountability of professionals, said, "Quite simply, if the buck doesn't stop with you, you're not a professional."

Professionalism also means behaving in an ethical manner, following ethical standards while carrying out responsibilities of everyday nursing work, every time, without fail (Rutledge, 2011). The ANA Code of Ethics (2008) describes the ethical obligations of the nurse. This ethical code was developed as a guide for nurses in carrying out their nursing responsibilities in a manner consistent with quality in nursing care and to meet the ethical obligations of the professional. The nine provisions of the ANA Code of Ethics are:

> *Provision 1—The nurse, in all professional relationships, practices with compassion and respect for the inherent dignity, worth, and uniqueness of every individual, unrestricted by considerations of social or economic status, personal attributes, or the nature of health problems.*
>
> *Provision 2—The nurse's primary commitment is to the patient, whether an individual, family, group, or community.*
>
> *Provision 3—The nurse promotes, advocates for, and strives to protect the health, safety, and rights of the patient.*
>
> *Provision 4—The nurse is responsible and accountable for individual nursing practice and determines the appropriate delegation of tasks consistent with the nurse's obligation to provide optimum patient care.*
>
> *Provision 5—The nurse owes the same duties to self as to others, including the responsibility to preserve integrity and safety, to maintain competence, and to continue personal and professional growth.*

Provision 6—*The nurse participates in establishing, maintaining, and improving healthcare environments and conditions of employment conducive to the provision of quality health care and consistent with the values of the profession through individual and collective action.*

Provision 7—*The nurse participates in the advancement of the profession through contributions to practice, education, administration, and knowledge development.*

Provision 8—*The nurse collaborates with other health professionals and the public in promoting community, national, and international efforts to meet health needs.*

Provision 9—*The profession of nursing, as represented by associations and their members, is responsible for articulating nursing values, for maintaining the integrity of the profession and its practice and for shaping social policy.*

However, professionalism in nursing is more than meeting the generally agreed-upon attributes listed above. Teamwork and collaboration, caring and compassion, and professional appearance are additional interesting attributes to be considered necessary for professionalism in nursing. Professionalism is visible when nurses provide care to and collaborate with patients, families, communities, nursing colleagues, and other members of the health care team. The complexity of today's health care environment demands teamwork and collegiality among health care professionals. This interprofessional collaboration, when multiple health care workers from different professional backgrounds work together, contributes to higher quality and safer patient care (WHO, 2010). These different healthcare professionals must communicate and interact with each other and respect the knowledge and skills that each professional brings to the team. The Institute of Medicine's "Future of Nursing" (2011) report recommended that nurses practice to the full extent of their education and training and be full partners with other health care professionals in redesigning health care in the United States. The professionalism of each clinician is central to the future of health care.

Caring is central to professional nursing and takes place every time a nurse-to-patient contact is made. Watson's "theory of caring" (1997) says the goal of nursing is to help the patient gain a higher degree of harmony within the mind, body, and soul, leading to an optimal state of health. This harmony is achieved through caring transactions. Compassion, empathy, and respect for human dignity are higher levels of caring and build on these caring transactions that occur at every interaction. True professionalism in nursing is seen when a nurse is able to balance the art and science of nursing; caring with competence.

Finally, a discussion of professionalism in nursing would be incomplete without some mention of professional appearance. Many nurses have shed their white uniforms and caps for the comfort and cleanliness of scrub attire. However, recent interest in the professional appearance of nurses has surged in organizations and among nurses. Because of the emphasis on the interprofessional team in health care as described above, it is often difficult to identify a nurse when most health care workers wear the same clothing, and identification badges have no titles on them. Many organizations have added the "RN" title as an appendage to identification badges. In addition, there has been a strong and proud movement in organizations for nurses to all wear the same color of scrub uniforms in order to distinguish the nurse from other caregivers.

The challenges to nursing professionalism today are as great as they have ever been. Nursing membership in professional and specialty organizations has declined over the last 30 years, and nurses question the professional value of those memberships. Yet, every nurse's practice is governed by the standards, code of ethics, and position statements developed by those professional groups to increase and define the professionalism of the discipline. The long-standing discourse surrounding the various pathways into nursing continues to challenge the professionalism of nursing. An interesting solution to this conundrum was recently proposed in the Institute of Medicine's "Future of Nursing" report. One of the key messages of the report stated that "nurses should achieve higher levels of education and training through an improved education system that promotes seamless academic progression," and added a specific recommendation that the proportion of nurses with baccalaureate degrees should be increased by 80% by 2020 (Institute of Medicine, 2011). This solution does not take away the various pathways into nursing, but clearly states the need for nurses to have a higher level of education for today's complex health care.

The quest for professionalism is also seen in today's hotly debated question of the autonomy of nursing practice. The debate rages at all levels of nursing but is most visible as advanced-practice nurses diligently fight to practice to the full extent of their education and training. Advanced-practice nurses are constantly challenged by licensing laws and practice regulations governing nursing's scope of practice, which vary from state to state and limit what nurses in different states are permitted by law to do (Institute of Medicine, 2011). This consequently challenges the autonomy of nurses to self-regulate, and hence their professionalism.

A final challenge to professionalism for nursing is found in the nature of the work of nursing, with shift hours, environmental health risks, stress and burnout, and the undervaluing of the contribution of nurses to healthcare. The Robert Wood Johnson Foundation (RWJF) wanted to know if nurses are viewed as key decision-makers to influence health care reform. Gallup surveyed more than 1,500 thought leaders from insurance, corporate, health services, government, and industry spheres, as well as university faculty.

The survey found that these leaders see nurses as trusted sources of information who have a great deal of influence on key elements of a quality health care system, including reducing medical errors, improving patient safety, and increasing the quality of patient care. However, when asked how much influence various professions and groups are likely to have in health care reform efforts, opinion leaders put nurses behind government, insurance and pharmaceutical executives, and other groups, citing lack of nursing leadership in health care (Gallup, 2010).

SUMMARY

Professionalism in nursing practice is a commitment to caring; competence and lifelong learning; strong ethical values; a pursuit of autonomy, accountability, and responsibility for practice; the demonstration of collaboration and collegiality; and the discovery and application of knowledge (Girard, Linton, and Besner, 2005). The Institute of Medicine's "Future of Nursing" report focuses on the need for nurses to be highly educated and contributing professionals in the healthcare workforce. The fact that the nurse has consistently been rated as the most trusted professional is meaningful and important to this discussion. Fundamental to nursing professionalism is the ability to show caring and competence in a manner to be worthy of and engender the continued trust and confidence of the public in our profession. Strategies that promote a commitment to nursing professionalism must be embraced by the profession and enthusiastically supported by other members of the health care team, including health care administrators and policy makers. The question of professionalism in nursing, still on a quest or finally accomplished, should be put to rest.

References

American Nurses Association. *A Seat at the Table: 50 Years of Progress. Compiled by Joni Ketter.* Silver Spring, MD: American Nurses Association; 1996.

American Nurses Association. *Professional Role Competence.* Silver Spring, MD: ANA; 2008. Available online at http://www.nursingworld.org/MainMenuCategories/Policy-Advocacy/Positions-and-Resolutions/ANAPositionStatements/Position-Statements-Alphabetically/Professional-Role-Competence.html. Accessed on April 1, 2013.

American Nurses Association. *Code of Ethics for Nurses with Interpretative Statements.* 2nd ed. Silver Spring, MD: Nursesbooks.org; 2001. Available online at http://www.nursingworld.org/MainMenuCategories/Ethics Standards/CodeofEthicsforNurses/Code-of-Ethics.pdf. Accessed on April 1, 2013.

American Nurses Association. *Nursing's Social Policy Statement: The Essence of the Profession.* 2nd ed. Silver Spring, MD: Nursesbooks.org; 2010a.

American Nurses Association. *Nursing: Scope and Standards of Practice.* 2nd ed. Silver Spring, MD: Nursesbooks.org; 2010b.

Brown EL. *Nursing for the Future.* New York: Russell Sage Foundation; 1948.

Cary AH. Certified registered nurses: Results of the study of the certified workforce. *Am J Nurs.* 2001;101:44–52.

Deans A, Austin A. *The History of the Farrand Training School for Nurses.* Detroit: Alumnae Association of the Farrand Training School for Nurses; 1936.

Flexner A. *Medical Education in the United States and Canada.* New York: Carnegie Foundation for the Advancement of Teaching; 1910.

Gallup. *Nursing Leadership from Bedside to Boardroom: Opinion Leaders' Perceptions.* Princeton, NJ: Robert Wood Johnson Foundation; 2010. Accessed at http://www.rwjf.org/content/dam/web-assets/2010/01/nursing-leadership-from-bedside-to-boardroom. Accessed on April 1, 2013.

Girard F, Linton N, Besner J. *Professional practice in nursing: A framework.* Nursing Leadership On-line Exclusive.2005.

Goldmark J. *Nursing and Nursing Education in the United States.* New York: Macmillan and Co.; 1923.

Hall RH. Professionalization and bureaucratization. *Am Sociological Rev.* 1968;33: 92–104.

Hendelman W. *Medicine and professionalism. 2009.* Ottawa, CA: University of Ottawa; 2009. Accessed at www.intermed.med.uottawa.ca ON April 1, 2013.

Institute of Medicine. *The Future of Nursing: Leading Change, Advancing Health.* Washington,DC: National Academies of Science; 2011.

Kalisch P, Kalisch B. *The Advance of American Nursing.* Philadelphia: J. B. Lippincott Company; 1995.

Nightingale F. *Notes on Nursing.* London: Harrison & Sons; 1860.

Polifko K. *The Practice Environment of Nursing: Issues and Trends.* Clifton Park,NY: Delmar Cengage Learning; 2011.

Registered Nurses' Association of Ontario. *Professionalism in Nursing.* Toronto: Registered Nurses' Association of Ontario; 2007.

Rutledge A. Define professionalism.2011. Accessed online at http://designprofessionalism.com/defining-design-professionalism-1.php. Accessed on April 1, 2031.

Styles M, Schumann M, Bickford C, White K. *Specialization and Credentialing in Nursing Revisited: Understanding the Issues, Advancing the Profession.* Silver Spring, MD: Nursebooks.org; 2008.

Turkoski B. Professionalism as ideology: a socio-historical analysis of the discourse of professionalism in nursing. *Nursing Inquiry.* 1995;2(2):83–89.

United States Public Health Service. *Fifty Years at the Division of Nursing.* Rockville,MD: United States Public Health Service; 1997.

Watson J. The theory of human caring: Retrospective and prospective. *Nurs Sci Q.* 1997;10(1):49–52.

White K, O'Sullivan A. *Essential Guide to Nursing Practice: Application of Scope and Standard of Practice.* Silver Spring, MD: Nursebooks.org; 2012.

Wilensky HL. The professionalization of everyone? *Am J Sociology.* 1964;70: 137–158.

World Health Organization. *Framework for Action on Interprofessional Education and Collaborative Practice.* Geneva: World Health Organization; 2010. Accessed at http://www.who.int/hrh/resources/framework_action/en/ Accessed on April 1, 2013.

Wuest J. Professionalism and the evolution of nursing as a discipline: a feminist perspective. *J Prof Nurs.* 1994;10(6):357–367.

Wynd C. Current factors contributing to professionalism in nursing. *J Prof Nurs.* 2003;19(5):251–261.

Chapter 7

Public Health: The "Population" as Patient

LAWRENCE O. GOSTIN

This chapter explores the vital importance of the health, safety, and well-being of the population, demonstrating that safeguarding the public's health requires a partnership between public health and clinical professionals. First, the chapter defines public health law, explaining its key characteristics. Second, it shows how law can be a tool for the public's health, offering several paradigms for the use of law to advance public health. Third, it shows how public health laws are often antiquated and draws attention to model laws and Institute of Medicine's guidance for modernizing public health statutes. Finally, the chapter shows how public health and clinical practice can have important synergies, recommending a closer integration of primary care and population health.

DEFINING FEATURES OF A DYNAMIC FIELD

The public health enterprise is concerned primarily with the safety and well-being of populations. The field of medicine, particularly its primary-care sector, also has a population-based perspective, but chiefly is concerned with the health of individual patients.

In medicine, physicians must do what is best for their individual patient, while also considering the health of the community. Public health has a different priority, focusing on interventions to improve and maintain the health of a wider population. Inherent in this approach is the reality that sometimes the government will require that individual rights be sacrificed for the greater good; people may have to forgo a certain amount of individual freedom, privacy, and autonomy in order to benefit their community. With this in mind, I have defined public health law as:

> The legal powers and duties of the state, in collaboration with its partners (e.g., health care, business, the community, the media, and academe), to assure the conditions for people to be healthy (e.g., to identify, prevent, and ameliorate risks to health in the population) and the limitations on the power of the state to constrain the autonomy, privacy, liberty, proprietary, or other legally protected interests of individuals for the common good. The prime objective of public health law is to pursue the highest possible level of physical and mental health in the population, consistent with the values of social justice. (Gostin, 2008)

This multifaceted definition focuses on five essential characteristics (Institute of Medicine, 2002 and 2011a):

(1) *Government*—The primary responsibility of safeguarding the public's health falls to the government, as it is best situated to act in the interests of the populace.
(2) *Populations*—Public health's goal is to improve the health and well-being of a group, rather than individual patients.
(3) *Relationships*—Public health is concerned with the relationship between the state and the people. Sometimes this

relationship justifies the government's imposition of burdens on individuals in order to promote the population's
greater good.

(4) *Services*—Public health improves the welfare of a group
by providing population-based services, grounded in the
scientific methodologies of public health (e.g., biostatistics
and epidemiology).

(5) *Power*—In order to promote the public's health, the government must possess certain powers to regulate and
control individuals and businesses. Since public health
often requires individual sacrifice, the government cannot rely on requests for voluntary cooperation; an ample,
yet clearly delineated power to coerce is required.

Law is the mechanism through which government can fulfill its
obligations to protect the public's health. The next section outlines
seven models of legal intervention, demonstrating how law can be
a tool to safeguard and promote the public's health. In each model,
the law (through constitutions, legislation, regulation, or the courts)
gives government the power to influence human behavior.

LAW AS A TOOL TO PROTECT THE PUBLIC'S HEALTH

Tax and Spend

One of the fundamental governmental powers, contained in the
federal and state constitutions, is the ability to tax and spend. The
power to spend allows the government to devote resources towards
vital public health infrastructure (Institute of Medicine, 2012a).
Government must hire and train a public health workforce, create

information and communication systems, conduct disease surveillance, maintain laboratory facilities, and establish the capacity to respond to public health emergencies.

Government can also use its spending power to influence policy and behavior. The Supreme Court of the United States has, for example, upheld a requirement to set a minimum drinking age of 21 as a condition of receiving federal highway funds (*South Dakota v. Dole*, 1987). However, in its recent landmark decision on the Affordable Care Act (ACA, "Obamacare"), the Court ruled that Congress could not set punitive conditions on funding by removing all Medicaid support as retaliation for failure to significantly expand coverage (*National Federation of Independent Business v. Sebelius*, 2012; Gostin, 2012).

The power to tax can also be used as a tool to influence the behavior of individuals and businesses. Taxes on unhealthy or harmful behaviors serve as a disincentive to engage in those activities. Many governments tax risky behaviors, such as smoking, in an effort to make it less attractive. Policymakers have similarly debated the idea of a tax on sugary soft drinks or other unhealthy foods. These types of monetary disincentives can be a powerful means of discouraging unhealthy behaviors, especially among young people. Tax relief can also be used as a positive incentive for engaging in healthful behaviors. A tax rebate or deduction, for example, is offered for purchasing health insurance or for income devoted to medical expenses.

The Informational Environment

Information influences the health-related choices that people make. Government can influence the informational environment, thus encouraging healthy behaviors and discouraging harmful behaviors. The government can engage in direct information dissemination through the use of educational campaigns. The law can impose product-labeling rules, requiring the inclusion of important information such as health warnings, nutritional information, or safe-use instructions. Governments can also impose outright bans on advertising, especially for information that is misleading or promotes unreasonably harmful products such as tobacco or alcohol.

Of course, by regulating or banning certain kinds of commercial speech, government is restricting businesses' freedom of expression. The Constitution enshrines the right to free speech as a core social value. However, there is a difference between expressing one's social or political views and engaging in commercial speech for profit. The tension between commercial speech and public health is apparent. The judiciary in the United States, for example, is deciding (as of this writing) whether the Food and Drug Administration (FDA) can require tobacco companies to display graphic health images on cigarette packages—a case likely to go to the Supreme Court.

The Built Environment

The environment in which one lives can have an immense impact on one's health. Government regulates workplace safety to reduce injuries. Cities require builders to comply with specific fire and building codes. Government also restricts the production and use of harmful environmental agents such as lead paint, asbestos, and pollution.

One of the most controversial uses of the built environment is to prevent chronic diseases caused by unhealthy diets and physical activity. City planners can include parks and playgrounds that encourage active lifestyles. Government can facilitate access to nutritional foods by encouraging the production of supermarkets in previously underserved areas. Laws can restrict the use of harmful products, such as cigarettes and alcohol. For example, many jurisdictions have banned smoking in all public spaces (Perdue et al., 2003).

The Socioeconomic Environment

Research indicates a clear correlation between socioeconomic status (SES) and health. Populations with the fewest financial, educational, and occupational resources generally are the least healthy. People of low SES are subject to a disproportionate number of harms, including: reduced access to material goods (food, shelter, and health care); a toxic physical environment; psychosocial stressors (financial, occupational, and social insecurity); and social contexts that promote risky behaviors. Governments can work to alleviate these specific determinants of morbidity and premature mortality, keeping in mind that social equality might be the ultimate way to promote the health of an entire population (Lynch et al., 2004).

Direct Regulation

The government has the power to regulate individuals, professions, and businesses, creating enforceable rules to protect the health and safety of workers, consumers, and the population at large. On the individual level, regulation can reduce injuries and death by controlling behavior. For example, in most places it is illegal to drive without a seatbelt (or bike without a helmet) or to drive while under the influence of drugs or alcohol. On the professional level, governments regulate the quality and standards of practice by requiring licenses and permits to enter a professional field. In the area of health, this power is used to regulate physicians' licenses, as well as to certify hospitals and nursing homes.

The classic form of public health regulation is to control the spread of infectious diseases, such as by testing, contact tracing, isolation, and quarantine. More controversial is the regulation of food and beverages. New York, for example, banned large serving sizes of sugary soft drinks in 2012, causing a political uproar (this was overturned in New York's supreme court in 2013, however).

Indirect Regulation Through the Tort System

The tort system aims to hold individuals and businesses civilly accountable for engaging in dangerous or harmful activities. Tort litigation can redress many kinds of public health problems. Companies that pollute or use toxic substances can be held liable for the environmental damage and adverse health effects that they have caused. Similarly, companies that produce dangerous products can be forced to compensate victims injured by their merchandise. The single most important public health litigation has perhaps been that against the tobacco industry, notably the 1998 settlement between tobacco companies and states totaling $206 billion in damages and penalties over 27 years. Other kinds of litigation have not fared so well, such as firearms lawsuits as well as food product lawsuits. Both firearms and certain food products can be dangerous, and industry claims can be misleading, but courts have been reluctant to find liability.

Deregulation

While law gives the government the power to protect the public's health, law can also serve as an impediment to this goal. In such cases, deregulation can be a useful tool. Politically popular policies, such as banning drug addicts' needle exchanges, can actually increase the spread of HIV and other blood-borne infections. Similarly, the criminalization of sexual acts performed by HIV-positive individuals (without disclosure) can serve as a disincentive for individuals to get tested or seek medical treatment.

PUBLIC HEALTH LAW REFORM

The laws relating to public health are scattered across count-less statutes and regulations at multiple levels of government. Problems of antiquity, inconsistency, redundancy, and ambiguity often render these laws ineffective, or even counterproductive, in advancing the population's health (Institute of Medicine, 2011a). In particular, health codes frequently are outdated, built up in layers over different periods of time, and highly fragmented among sub-national political units. Some states have made efforts to modernize their public health laws, but many are still plagued by these problems.

Problem of Antiquity

The most striking characteristic of state public health laws, and the one that underlies many of their defects, is their overall antiquity. Certainly, some statutes are relatively recent in origin, such as those relating to emerging health threats based on the Model State Emergency Health Powers Act (Gostin et al., 2002). However, a great deal of public health law was framed in the late nineteenth and early to mid–twentieth century and contains elements that are 40 to 100 years old, such as infectious disease law. Old laws are not necessarily bad laws, but they can impede effective public health functioning, such as by failing to have the necessary powers and safeguards needed to meet modern threats.

Problem of Multiple Layers of Law

Related to the problem of antiquity is the problem of multiple layers of law. The law usually consists of successive layers of statutes and amendments, built up in some cases over 100 years or more in response to existing or perceived health threats. This is particularly troublesome in the area of infectious diseases, which forms a substantial part of state health codes. Because communicable-disease laws have been passed piecemeal in response to specific epidemics, they tell the story of the history of disease control (e.g., smallpox, yellow fever, cholera, tuberculosis, venereal diseases, polio, and AIDS).

Problem of Inconsistency

Public health laws remain fragmented, not only within specific jurisdictions, but among them as well. Health codes in various states have evolved independently, leading to profound variations in the structure, substance, and procedures for detecting, controlling, and preventing injury and disease. In fact, statutes and regulations can vary so significantly in definitions, methods, age, and scope that they defy orderly categorization.

Public health law, therefore, should be reformed so that it conforms to modern scientific and legal standards, is more consistent within and among states, and is more uniform in its approach to different health threats. Rather than making artificial distinctions among diseases, public health interventions should be based primarily on the degree of risk, the cost and efficacy of the response, and the burdens on human rights. A single set of standards and procedures would add needed clarity and coherence to legal regulation, and would reduce the opportunity for politically motivated disputes about how to classify newly emergent health threats. The "Turning Point" Model Public Health Act provides a useful guide to states seeking to reform their laws (Hodge et al., 2006)—a point underscored by the Institute of Medicine (2011a).

MEDICINE AND PUBLIC HEALTH: THE SYNERGIES

Although they may have different priorities, both medicine and public health are concerned with the population's health. Consequently, it is vitally important to ensure there are synergies between the two fields. A recent Institute of Medicine report (Institute of Medicine, 2012b), for example, explores the points of integration between medicine and public health (Landon et al., 2012). Health education campaigns, such as the recent "Million Hearts" Initiative, can support clinical advice given by primary care professionals regarding smoking, alcohol, food, and physical activity. At the same time, public health and primary care professionals can share information. Clinicians can report vital information to assist public health agencies in monitoring health threats in the population (Institute of Medicine, 2011b).

At the same time, agencies can keep clinicians and their patients well informed. For example, in 2006, New York City implemented a novel response to the diabetes epidemic, including: mandatory laboratory reporting of glycosylated, best practice recommendations for health care professionals on glycemic control, and information and resources on diabetes management for patients.

Many clinical practices can have profound effects on a population's health, requiring close coordination among health care and public health professionals. A clear illustration is the problem of hospital-acquired infections, as well as physician over-prescribing antibiotics. In both cases, inappropriate clinical management can drive the spread of drug-resistant infections, which is a major public health threat.

Law and policy have tried, with variable success, to create stronger ties between primary care and public health. The Affordable

Care Act, for example, has numerous provisions that seek to improve clinical practice to benefit the public's health:

(1) a Prevention and Public Health Fund, a Preventive Services Task Force, and a "Creating Healthier Communities" flexible grant program to expand the nation's investment in prevention and wellness;

(2) incentives for prevention and wellness by eliminating cost-sharing for primary care services in Medicare, Medicaid, and qualified health plans;

(3) funding for public health workforce improvement; and

(4) performance measures, creating demonstration programs to evaluate evidence-based clinical practices and translating research into effective programs.

Congress has gutted many of these public health provisions, but the ACA demonstrates the potential synergies between public health and health care (Hardcastle et al., 2011).

CONCLUSION

Although physicians often view the patient, who presents with an illness or injury, as their principal concern, public health officials view the population as "the patient." This requires intervening at the population, rather than the individual, level. It means ensuring the conditions in which people can be healthy, living in decent and safe communities. The conditions for population health range from nutritious food, clean water, sanitation, disease vector abatement, and tobacco control, to the built environment and the deeper socio-economic determinants of health. The legal and regulatory tools entail economic incentives for healthy behavior or disincentives for risk behavior, information and education, direct and indirect regulation, and sometimes deregulation.

The population-based approach is not callous to the plight of each individual, but acts for the society as a whole. Sometimes this requires stopping individuals or businesses from harming others—directly or indirectly. And sometimes it requires paternalistic rules that discourage individuals from harming themselves; for example, from smoking; consuming excess sugar, fat, or sodium; or a sedentary lifestyle. Because public health operates at this social level, it is inherently political—balancing individual rights and interests against the common good. Because it is political, it is also deeply controversial, but of enduring importance to people, communities, and all of society.

References

Gostin LO. The Supreme Court's historic ruling on the Affordable Care Act: economic sustainability and universal coverage. *JAMA.* 2012;308(6):571–572. doi:10.1001/jama.2012.906

Gostin LO. *Public Health Law: Power, Duty, Restraint.* 2nd ed. Berkeley: University of California Press; 2008.

Gostin LO et al. The Model State Emergency Health Powers Act: Planning and response to bioterrorism and naturally occurring infectious diseases. *JAMA.* 2002;288:622–628.

Hardcastle LE, Record KL, Jacobson PD, et al. Improving the population's health: the Affordable Care Act and the importance of integration. *J Law, Med & Ethics.* 2011;39(3):317–327.

Hodge JG, Gostin LO, Gebbie K, et al. Transforming public health law: The Turning Point Model State Public Health Act. *J Law, Med & Ethics.* 2006;33(4):77–84.

Institute of Medicine. *The Future of the Public's Health in the Twenty-first Century.* Washington, DC: National Academy Press; 2002.

Institute of Medicine. *For the Public's Health: Revitalizing Law and Policy to Meet New Challenges.* Washington, DC: National Academy Press; 2011a.

Institute of Medicine. *For the Public's Health: The Role of Measurement in Action and Accountability.* Washington, DC: National Academy Press; 2011b.

Institute of Medicine. *For the Public's Health: Investing in a Healthier Future.* Washington, DC: National Academy Press; 2012a.

Institute of Medicine. *Primary Care and Public Health: Exploring Integration to Improve Population Health.* Washington, DC: National Academy Press; 2012b.

Landon BE, Grumbach K, Wallace, PJ. Integrating public health and primary care systems. *JAMA.* 2012, 308(5): 461–62.

Lynch, Smith, Harper, et al. Is income inequality a determinant of population health? A systematic review. *Millbank Q.* 2004;82:5–99.

National Federation of Independent Business v. Sebelius, 567 U.S. _ (2012).

Perdue, W. C., Stone, L. A., & Gostin, L. O. (2003). The built environment and its relationship to the public's health: The legal framework. *AJPH,* 93(9), 1390–1394.

South Dakota v. Dole, 483 U.S. 203 (1987).

Chapter 8

Exploring the Role of Law and Legal Systems in the Therapeutic Relationship

JAMES G. HODGE

Professionalism in the treatment and care of patients is molded by multiple factors, including law and policy. Obligations and responsibilities of physicians, nurses, and other practitioners to their patients are shaped by all types of laws (e.g., constitutional, statutory, regulatory, judicial) at every level of government (e.g., national, state, tribal, local). Corresponding policies among hospitals, insurers, and other health institutions set additional professionalism benchmarks. Practitioners' failures to adhere to laws, policies, and medical ethics carry their own legal consequences, including exposure to liability, sanctions, and licensure investigations. Precisely how the law affects therapeutic relationships directly and indirectly through health systems fluctuates. Over the centuries, legal principles and systems have evolved to incorporate state-of-the-art developments in medicine, public health, nursing, research, and health care delivery. From these reforms emerges a unifying role of law in simultaneously facilitating and constraining therapeutic relationships. This chapter explores this dynamic through an examination of legal tensions in professionalism and patient care in select, key policy areas, including direct regulation of health care practitioners, health care system reforms, patient autonomy, informed consent, privacy, and end-of-life issues.

LEGAL PROFESSIONALISM AMONG PRACTITIONERS

Not long ago, practitioner–patient relationships began typically when a patient physically presented herself or himself for examination or treatment at a clinician's office, hospital, or other health care setting. Meeting and examining an individual for medical purposes was the primary basis for establishing a therapeutic relationship. Antiquated laws in some states continue to reflect the notion that physical encounters with patients are quintessential to generating therapeutic relationships. Some states' laws, for example, still refer to in-person examinations as a precept to physician–patient relationships (Hodge et al., 2008, pp. 23–28).

In reality, the legal question of "who is a patient" is changing. Increasing numbers of state legislatures and courts concur that practitioner–patient relationships, and corresponding practitioner duties, can arise (or continue, once established) in unconventional ways. Telephone consultations, email or other online exchanges, and even outside clinical reviews via "telemedicine" can give rise to therapeutic relationships legally. No matter how they arise, once these relationships are established, practitioners are bound by law to abide by specific norms in providing care to patients until the relationship terminates. The law directly impacts professionalism in patient care by authorizing licensure of practitioners and entities, defining practitioners' scope of practice, setting the appropriate standard of care, and assessing liability.

Licensure of Practitioners and Health Care Institutions

All states statutorily authorize the licensure of physicians, nurses, and other health practitioners and of health care facilities (e.g., hospitals, clinics, nursing homes, long-term care facilities, and hospice care). Concerning practitioner licensing, despite calls for national standards, there are no uniform licensing qualifications. Medical licenses tied to professional standards of education, training, and knowledge vary extensively across states. As a result, physicians licensed in one state cannot practice in others, except pursuant to licensure-reciprocity laws in declared emergencies, telemedicine applications, or other narrow exceptions. Nurses face the same stricture, although they may enjoy interjurisdictional licensure in over half the states that endorse the Nurse Licensure Compact (NLC) (National Council of State Boards of Nursing, 2000). Absent specific legal mechanisms to extend licensure across state lines, practitioners face civil or criminal penalties if they practice outside their authorized jurisdictions. Despite the availability of electronic and other media designed to bridge patients and practitioners together, states' traditional licensure restrictions can sometimes derail therapeutic relationships solely because the patient lives outside the practitioner's jurisdiction.

Scope of Practice

A practitioner's license is more than a ticket to practice a profession. Legal licensing standards and routine board reviews require proof of practitioners' skills, conduct, and responsibilities as part of therapeutic relationships. Through licenses, state legislatures and regulatory agencies define legally the appropriate scope of practice for each medical and nursing professional. "Scope of practice" refers to the extent of a practitioner's ability to provide health services pursuant to her or his competence and license, certification, privileges, or other lawful authority to practice (Agency for Healthcare Research and Quality, 2005; Wise, 2008; Lewandowski and Adamle, 2009). Scope-of-practice limits within the therapeutic relationship are intended largely to protect patients. For example, registered nurses (and nurse practitioners in some states) may legally issue nursing diagnoses for patients but generally cannot provide clinical diagnoses like a physician can. Clinical diagnoses exceed a nurse's scope of practice. In this way, practitioners' roles and services to the patient are limited via law, even if the delivery of such services may benefit patients in some cases.

Medical and Legal Standards of Care

Practicing within a professional's scope does not itself ensure quality or appropriate care for patients. Health practitioners must also adhere to the prevailing standard of care. Although sometimes conflated, medical and legal standards of care are different. *Medical standards of care* describe the type and level of medical care required by professional norms and requirements, as well as institutional objectives (Agency for Healthcare Research and Quality, 2005; Hick et al., 2009; Pegalis, 2009). A medical standard of care varies among different types of medical facilities, based on prevailing circumstances (Hick et al., 2009). *Legal standards of care* refer to the minimum amount of care and skill a practitioner must exercise based on what a reasonable and prudent practitioner would do in similar circumstances (Mastroianni, 2006; Dobbs, 2000; *Hood v. Phillips*, 1977).

Legal standards of care are necessarily fact-specific, flexible, and subject to differing interpretations nationally (Dobbs, 2000). They may approximate medical standards, but not always. Courts, for example, may determine that prevailing medical practices are insufficient or unacceptable. In one famous case (*Helling v. Carey*, 1974), a court determined that existing medical guidance for glaucoma screening was insufficient, allowing an injured patient to recover damages against a clinician who failed to screen, even though the prevailing medical standard of care did not require it at the time.

A result of the case was the incorporation of routine glaucoma testing for older patients within the medical standard of care.

Liability

As in *Helling* and other judicial decisions, failing to meet the legal standard of care can result in claims of liability, usually grounded in medical malpractice (a.k.a. "medmal") against physicians, nurses, other practitioners, and health care entities. Although often purported by patient advocates and plaintiff's attorneys to be essential to patient safety and quality of care, medmal liability has engendered considerable controversy over decades. Federal and state tort reforms designed to rein in astronomical medmal awards imply that successful claims are rampant. In reality, most medmal claims are either unwarranted (and summarily dismissed) or settled out of court for a fraction of the alleged damages to the patient. Still, the specter of health care liability alters the therapeutic relationship through practitioners' demand for consistent, repeated, and sometimes excessive medical tests and other maneuvers designed more to protect themselves from medmal claims than to advance patients' health. Explicit liability protections have been increasingly considered and enacted via federal and state laws, especially concerning declared emergencies when practitioners must triage patients under a crisis standard of care (Committee on Guidance, 2012).

THE EVOLVING LEGAL STRUCTURE
UNDERLYING HEALTH CARE DELIVERY
AND PROFESSIONALISM

Laws not only directly affect professionalism in patient care, they significantly shape the health care system in which these relationships arise and are regulated. At the state and local levels, governments routinely frame the delivery of health care services via statutory, regulatory, and judicial laws. Each year, state legislators enact numerous state bills that dictate the type of care practitioners must provide, how much they can charge, the bases on which patients are insured, and how health care and insurance entities are organized. Permissive state laws during the 1980s, for example, ushered in a new era of managed care that continues to shape practitioners' provision of structured health services to patients (Furrow et al., 2008).

At the federal level, laws regulating health care delivery enacted since the New Deal in the 1930s have had a profound impact on professionalism in health care. Notable federal legislative milestones include the introduction of Medicare and Medicaid programs via the Social Security Act Amendments of 1965 (Social Security Amendments, 1965), the transition to employer-based insurance facilitated by the Employee Retirement Income Security Act (ERISA, 1974), the curbing of hospital "patient dumping" via the Emergency Medical Treatment and Active Labor Act in 1986 (EMTALA, 1986), and the expansion of insurance availability through the Health Insurance Portability and Accountability Act of 1996 (HIPAA, 1996). These and numerous other federal statutes and regulations have shifted the therapeutic relationship into a modern era of corporate health care models that arguably have led to greater efficiencies in health care service delivery.

Despite these patchwork legal reforms, health economists and others have warned for years that the health care system is underperforming and unsustainable (Reinhardt, 2012). Patients' lack of access to care and spiraling costs in the health care system present unique public health problems. Millions who are uninsured or underinsured fail to seek preventive or other care until they must have it, often bankrupting themselves along the way. Patients' inability to access health services has become a leading cause of preventable morbidity and mortality in the United States (Institute of Medicine, 2009). After numerous failed attempts since the 1950s to comprehensively reform the health care system, the Patient Protection and Affordable Care Act was enacted on March 23, 2010 (PPACA, 2010). Among its voluminous goals, PPACA will require (by 2014) most individuals to acquire or maintain basic health insurance (a.k.a. "individual mandate") and force insurers to cover persons regardless of their age or preexisting conditions (Group Health Plans, 2011). Coupled with potential significant expansions of Medicaid populations, unprecedented numbers of Americans may attain basic access to health services. For practitioners, the PPACA offers new opportunities to treat millions of new patients through long-standing therapeutic relationships supported by extended insurance coverage tied to employment or public insurance programs.

Although falling short of providing a "gold standard" of complete and comprehensive coverage, like other industrialized countries' national health systems, PPACA's "silver promise" may be tarnished by judicial and political challenges. In June 2012, the United States Supreme Court issued its Opinion regarding the constitutionality of two key provisions of the Act, specifically concerning the individual mandate provision and the expansion of state Medicaid programs via the federal power to tax and spend (*National Federation of Independent Business v. Sebelius*, 2012). While the Court rejected arguments that Congress's power to regulate interstate commerce supported a mandate to purchase health insurance, or any other product for that matter, it ultimately defended the individual mandate as a proper exercise of Congress's power to tax.

However, Congress's use of its spending power to require states to accept PPACA's new influx of Medicaid patients or lose all of their existing Medicaid funding was denounced as contrary to principles of federalism by the Court. As a result, expansion of Medicaid programs to extend care to millions of uninsured Americans is contingent upon states' acceptance of federal resources initially to fund care for new enrollees. Following the decision, some states suggested they would not accept PPACA's expansion of their Medicaid populations, although most probably will. Still, millions of prospective patients seeking access to basic health services through Medicaid face an uncertain future (Goodnough, 2012). Congressional Republicans and their 2012 presidential candidate, former Massachusetts governor Mitt Romney (despite his passing similar health care reforms in Massachusetts) have vowed consistently to repeal "Obamacare" (PPACA, 2010). Some state legislatures and executive agencies have initially refused to implement future portions of PPACA based on political disagreements.

Politics around PPACA are already affecting therapeutic relationships by dictating what sort of services insurance must cover, including contraceptives. PPACA directs all new group health plans to cover, without patient co-pays, a variety of preventative health services for women and others (42 U.S.C. § 300gg-13(a), 2006). The Health Resources and Services Administration (HRSA) is vested with authority to determine which preventative services must be covered (42 U.S.C. § 300gg-13(a)(4), 2006) depending on whether they will improve well-being or decrease the likelihood of targeted conditions (Institute of Medicine, 2011). HRSA's determination in January 2012 that most health insurance plans must cover most contraceptives and sterilization procedures for women (Health Resources and Services Administration, accessed 2012; U.S. Dept. of Health and Human Services [DHHS], 2012) led to immediate objections on theological grounds by Catholic and other religious entities. Ultimately, the Obama administration committed to allowing religious organizations to avoid paying directly for contraceptive services as long as their health insurance companies provide such services to women free of charge (Goodstein, 2012).

PROTECTING PATIENTS: THE ROLE OF THE PHYSICIAN, PATIENT, AND SOCIETY

One ethical pillar of the therapeutic relationship in the modern era is the need to protect patient autonomy against traditional acts of medical paternalism, except in special circumstances. Societal expectations of patient autonomy are captured, and in some cases advanced directly, through law. One of the foundations of patient autonomy, the principle of informed consent, is espoused prominently in judicial cases like *Schloendorff v. Society of New York Hospital*, a decision admonishing a New York clinician for failing to seek full patient consent prior to operating on her cancerous tumor (*Schloendorff v. Society of New York Hospital*, 1914). In *Canterbury v. Spence*, a federal district court clarified the role of patient informed consent as an essential part of the standard of care (*Canterbury*, 1972). States have since required patient informed consent explicitly via legislation and regulation, setting terms and conditions for its execution in clinical care and research (Federal Policy for the Protection of Human Subjects, 1991). Although an important component of the therapeutic relationship, modern execution of patient informed consent is questionable. Failures to properly obtain consent because of perfunctory, expedited forms or limits of patients' health literacy can negate intended benefits underlying the practice. Resulting liability claims against practitioners and hospitals continue to arise (*Spencer v. Goodill*, 2011).

Patients' Bill of Rights

Enhanced information is at the core of advancing patient autonomy. Health consumers today have online access to innumerable sources of medical information. Some of this information is trustworthy; some is quackery. Except for outright false or misleading claims, however, commercial entities have First Amendment rights to circulate medical information related to diagnoses, drugs, or products. Consumers' increasing reliance on commercial medical resources off the Web or via advertisements can skew the therapeutic relationship as patients demand medical care or services, whether or not they actually need them (Cassel and Guest, 2012).

Patients' expectation of information and related protections in how health services are delivered have been espoused through something akin to a "Bill of Rights." The American Hospital Association issued its version of a patients' bill of rights in 1973 (American Hospital Association, 1973), offering a non-binding description of what patients may reasonably expect while hospitalized (Annas, 1998). It included rights to considerate and respectful care, relevant and understandable treatment information, recommended treatments, and privacy. Additional patients' rights documents in other health care sectors followed (N.C. Gen. Stat. Ann. § 131E-117, 2012; National Institutes of Health, 2010; Hospice Association of America, accessed 2012). Nearly all these documents focus on patients' rights *in* health care rather than a right *to* health care (Annas, 1998).

While initially generated by health care sectors, patients' bills of rights have legal support. The Clinton Administration's 1997 health care reform proposal, for example, focused on patients' rights to access to information, privacy, and dignity. The only right *to* health care advanced in the proposal concerned access to emergency care, something the aforementioned EMTALA already provided (Advisory Commission on Consumer Protection and Quality in the Health Care Industry, 1997). More recently, a congressional proposal advocated a "patient bill of rights" for covered children through state Medicaid programs (ChiPACC Act, 2009; Medically Fragile Children's Act, 2009). The federal DHHS's "New Patient's Bill of Rights" via PPACA (U.S. Dep't of HHS, 2010) goes beyond mere guidance to help ensure patients' access to health insurance and nondiscriminatory services.

Privacy

Patient autonomy is also grounded in extant legal expressions of decisional, bodily, and informational privacy. Modern interpretations of constitutional law evince greater respect for patient autonomy and bodily privacy within the context of the therapeutic relationship. Since *Griswold v. Connecticut* (1965), which legalized access to contraceptives, the Supreme Court has advanced the scope of patients' decisional privacy via ordered principles of liberty inherent in substantive due process. In *Cruzan v. Missouri Department of Health* (1990), which involved the withdrawal of medical care from an adult vegetative patient, the Court framed a patient's right to refuse treatment pursuant to bodily privacy interests. Justice Sandra Day O'Connor explained: "The sanctity...and individual privacy of the human body [are] obviously fundamental to liberty. Every violation of a person's bodily integrity is an invasion of his or her liberty" (*Cruzan*, 1990). Provided a patient's wishes to reject life-sustaining care are backed by clear and convincing evidence, neither government nor health practitioners are positioned legally to continue care. *Cruzan* and its progeny, like the infamous Terry Schiavo case (*In re Guardianship of Schiavo*, 2001) and other decisions (*Blouin*, 2004; *Granato*, 2011) have led to expanded conceptions of bodily integrity under liberty principles rather than through more generalized privacy rights partially relied on in cases like *Roe v. Wade* (*Roe*, 1973).

Legal principles of health information privacy are similarly grounded in constitutional law. In *Whalen v. Roe* (1977), the Supreme Court affirmed a state public health reporting requirement against claims of health information privacy infringements. The Court noted, however, that individual privacy interests must be balanced against governments' interests in collecting health information. Supplementing this basic constitutional requirement are numerous health information privacy laws at all levels of government. The HIPAA Privacy Rule (HIPAA, 2002) and similar state laws provide detailed legal standards for how health professionals and others must assure and protect the privacy and security of patients' identifiable health data. Additional laws provide even greater protections for mental health, genetic, cancer, HIV/AIDS, and research data.

Patient privacy, however, is not considered an absolute under any of these laws. On the contrary; legal exceptions allow disclosures of health information without patient authorization to public health authorities, researchers, law enforcement, courts, and others. Against this legal backdrop, practitioners and patients alike are left to slog through a legal maze of privacy protections and exceptions to determine the breadth and extent of acquisitions, uses, and disclosures of health data through the therapeutic relationship (Gostin and Hodge, 2002).

END-OF-LIFE DECISIONS

End-of-life decisions are among the most sensitive and difficult for practitioners and patients alike. These decisions commence with the diagnosis of a patient's terminal condition, and only end with the patient's death. With so much at stake, the roles of practitioners and patients via the therapeutic relationship are complicated. The law simultaneously offers practitioners discretion as to the nature of their handling of patients facing terminal conditions, and equips patients with considerable authority to control their fates. Not surprisingly, inexorable conflicts arise. Instead of clear answers, sometimes all the law can do is provide paths to resolve these conflicts.

Advanced Directives

One legal pathway to facilitating patient end-of-life care is to empower patients with authority over decisions related to their ongoing care. Since the mid-1980s, states have legally constructed three predominant types of advance directives to protect end-of-life decision-making: "living wills," health care proxies/surrogates, and durable powers of attorney. Living wills allow patients to direct when and how they want treatments or sustenance to be administered or withheld. Through health care proxies, patients designate one or more persons to make end-of-life health care decisions for when they might lack competence or are incapable of making these decisions. Proxy indications are often combined with living wills.

An advance directive authorizing durable power of attorney allows the holder of the power to act for the patient, whether the patient is competent or incompetent. Variations of these models are numerous. Visitation declarations allow patients to designate which individuals are permitted to visit and in what priority (Jones, 1997). Psychiatric advance directives enable patients with fluctuating mental capacity to define in advance their acceptance or refusal of particular mental health treatments (National Resource Center, 2011). While advance directives can relieve practitioners from critical decisions on end-of-life care, some struggle to adhere to patients' wishes when their training, morality, and legal duties to provide care are contravened. In most cases, however, patient wishes legally override contrary attempts to provide medical treatment.

Palliative Care

Regardless of a patient's life expectancy, legal and ethical norms support their access to palliative care via health practitioners. *Palliative care* refers generally to medical interventions (e.g., painkillers, hospice care) to provide comfort for patients, rather than treat their underlying conditions (World Health Organization, 2012). Most clinicians embrace the need for strong palliative care, but they have legitimate legal concerns. Practitioners may fear that painkillers may hasten a terminal patient's death, subjecting the practitioner to potential liability, even though advance directives can legally absolve them of these concerns. Increasingly, failure to provide adequate palliative care to terminal patients may pose greater risks of legal liability grounded in malpractice, negligent and intentional infliction of emotional distress, patient abandonment, and elder-abuse (Baluss and Lee, 2003). One court in Virginia found that a physician fell below the standard of care when he failed to provide pain management "consistent with the level of the patient's suffering" (*Cook*, 2010).

Physician-Assisted Dying

Since the companion cases of *Vacco v. Quill* (1997) and *Washington v. Glucksberg* (1997), the Supreme Court has affirmed that terminal patients' liberty rights are not so broad as to require physicians to assist them with their dying. Compelling governmental interests in preserving life and the sanctity of the practice of medicine, among other concerns, outweigh a patient's interest in a dignified death through clinical assistance. In at least two states (Oregon and Washington), however, legislatures have authorized physician-assisted deaths for terminally ill patients under tight regulatory controls. The Montana Supreme Court has judicially authorized physician-assisted death in narrow cases (*Baxter*, 2009). In these jurisdictions, appropriately trained physicians are not required to provide such services, but rather are privileged to do so.

While patient uptake of physician-assisted dying or euthanasia in these states is extremely limited, practitioners increasingly may face a cascade of patient demands for dignified deaths, especially with emerging legal support for palliative care. Reconciling legal distinctions between affirmative acts that directly bring about death (generally disdained in the law) and failures or omissions to act, from which death ensues (generally favored, provided they are consistent with patients' wishes), is not easy. Within the therapeutic relationship, is there a meaningful difference between a physician who intentionally injects his willing patient with a substance to immediately end her life versus injecting the same patient with a painkiller that expedites her death? Ethicists disagree, but in most jurisdictions the law stands firm. In the former case, the physician is criminally liable; in the latter, she may simply be following the standard of care. At times, it seems a legal distinction without justification.

CONCLUSION

The role of law within the therapeutic relationship is profound, controversial, and politically charged. Law impacts health practitioners directly through licensure, scope of practice, standard of care, and liability provisions. Law impacts practitioners indirectly via regulations of the health care system through which patients are encountered, treated, and insured. Law promotes the autonomy of patients through informed consent protections; "patients' bills of rights;" and respect for decisional, bodily, and informational privacy interests. Law addresses end-of-life care through creation of advance directives, affirmation of palliative care, and general admonitions against physician-assisted dying. In these and additional areas at the heart of practitioner–patient relationships, lawmakers attempt to create effective policies by balancing practitioner and patient interests. Their objective is a moving target.

As societal changes and ever-rising demands on health care systems continue to shape therapeutic relationships, laws must increasingly reflect what it means to be a patient in the new age of medical practice; enhance practitioners' ability to treat patients efficiently and safely without limitations based solely on jurisdictional boundaries; continue to reform the health care system through which care is provided; and incorporate ethical and cultural norms that respect patient dignity without sacrificing practitioners' professional responsibilities to advance their patients' welfare. This last objective will prove particularly vexing as continued advances in medical science and services confront traditional conceptions of legal and ethical duties of practitioners and patients.

ACKNOWLEDGEMENTS

The author would like to acknowledge and thank the research, drafting, and editing assistance of Siena Smith, JD, MA; Leila Barraza, JD, MPH; Lexi C. White, JD, PhD candidate; and Lauren Burkhart, JD candidate, at the Sandra Day O'Connor College of Law, Arizona State University.

References

42 U.S.C. § 300gg-13(a) (2006).
42 U.S.C. § 300gg-13(a)(4) (2006).
Advisory Commission on Consumer Protection and Quality in the Health Care Industry. Consumer Bill of Rights and Responsibilities. November 1997.

Available at: http://www.hcqualitycommission.gov/cborr/. Accessed July 16, 2012.

Agency for Healthcare Research and Quality. *Altered Standards of Care in Mass Casualty Events: Bioterrorism and Other Public Health Emergencies.* Publication No. 05–0043. Rockville, MD: 2005.

American Hospital Association. *A Patient's Bill of Rights.* 1973. Available at: http://www.patienttalk.info/AHA-Patient_Bill_of_Rights.htm. Accessed July 16, 2012.

Annas GJ. A national bill of patients' rights. *N Engl J Med.* 1998;338: 695–700, 696.

Baluss ME, Lee KF. Legal consideration for palliative care in surgical practice. *J Am Coll Surg.* 2003;197(2):323–330, 327.

Baxter v. State, 354 Mont. 234, 224 P.3d 1211 (Mont. 2009).

Blouin ex rel. Estate of Pouliot v. Spitzer, 356 F.3d 348, 361 (2d Cir. 2004).

Canterbury v. Spence, 464 F.2d 772, 772 (D.C. Cir. 1972).

Cassel CK, Guest JA. Choosing wisely: helping physicians and patients make smart decisions about their care. *JAMA.* 2012;307(17):1801–1802.

ChiPACC Act of 2009, H.R. 722, 111th Cong. § 2(b).

Cook v. Hartford Life and Accident Insurance Co., CIV. A. 3:09–1002, 2010 WL 3259414 (S.D.W. Va. Aug. 18, 2010).

Cruzan by Cruzan v. Director, Missouri Dept. of Health, 497 U.S. 261, 279 FN 7, 342, 110 S. Ct. 2841, 2852, 111 L. Ed. 2d 224 (1990).

Dobbs D. *The Law of Torts.* St. Paul, MN: West Group; 2000.

Emergency Medical Treatment and Active Labor Act, 42 U.S.C. § 1395dd (1986).

Employee Retirement Income Security Act, 29 U.S.C. § 1002 (1974).

Federal Policy for the Protection of Human Subjects ("Common Rule"), 45 C.F.R. § 46 (1991).

Furrow BR, et al. *Health Law: Cases, Materials, and Problems.* 6th ed. St. Paul, MN: West Publishing; 2008.

Goodnough A. Lines are drawn over opting out of Medicaid plan. *New York Times,* July 12, 2012.

Goodstein L. Bishops were prepared for battle over birth control coverage. *New York Times,* Feb. 9, 2012.

Gostin LO, Hodge JG. Personal privacy and common goods: a framework for balancing under the National Health Information Privacy Rule. *Minn Law Rev.* 2002;86:1439–1480.

Granato v. City & County of Denver, 11-CV-00304-MSK-BNB, 2011 WL 3820730 (D. Colo. Aug. 30, 2011). Paramedics administered fluids to the patient despite the patient's statement that she did not want the treatment. Since the patient was competent to express a desire not to receive medical treatment, the court allowed her constitutional claim for violation of her bodily integrity to proceed.

Griswold v. Connecticut, 381 U.S. 479, 85 S. Ct. 1678, 14 L. Ed. 2d 510 (1965).

Group Health Plans and Health Insurance Issuers Relative to Coverage of Preventative Services Under PPACA, 76 *Fed Regist.* 46621–01 (August 3, 2011) (to be codified at 45 C.F.R. § 147.130).

Hanfling D et al., eds.; Committee on Guidance for Establishing Crisis Standards of Care for Use in Disaster Situations, Institute of Medicine of the National Academy's Crisis Standards of Care. *A Systems Framework for Catastrophic Disaster Response.* 2012.

Health Insurance Portability and Accountability Act, Pub. L. No. 104–191, 110 Stat. 1936 (1996).

Health Insurance Portability and Accountability Act ("Privacy Rule"), 45 C.F.R. § 160, 164 (2002).

Health Resources and Services Administration. Women's preventative services: required health plan coverage guidelines. Available at: http://www.hrsa.gov/womensguidelines/. Accessed July 16, 2012.

Helling v. Carey, 83 Wash. 2d 514, 519, 519 P.2d 981, 983 (1974).

Hick JL, Barbera JA, Kelen GD. Refining surge capacity: conventional, contingency, and crisis capacity. *Disaster Med Public Health Prep.* 2009;3:559.

Hodge JG, Pulver A, Hogben M, Bhattacharya D, Brown EF. Expedited partner therapy: assessing the legal environment. *Am J Public Health.* 2008;98(2):23–28.

Hood v. Phillips, 554 S.W.2d 160, 165 (Tex. 1977).

Hospice Association of America. Hospice patients' Bill of Rights. Available at: http://www.nahc.org/haa/attachments/BillOfRights.pdf Accessed July 16, 2012.

In re Guardianship of Schiavo, 780 So. 2d 176 (Fla. Dist. Ct. App. 2001).

Institute of Medicine. America's uninsured crisis: consequences for health and health care. February 23, 2009. Available at: http://www.iom.edu/Reports/2009/Americas-Uninsured-Crisis-Consequences-for-Health-and-Health-Care.aspx. Accessed July 16, 2012.

Institute of Medicine, Board on Population Health and Health Practice. Clinical preventative services for women: closing the gaps. July 19, 2011. Available at: http://iom.edu/Reports/2011/Clinical-Preventive-Services-for-Women-Closing-the-Gaps.aspx. Accessed July 16, 2012.

Jones CJ. Decision making at the end of life. 63 *Am Jur Trials* 1, § 27 (Originally published in 1997; database updated March 2012).

Lewandowski W, Adamle K. Substantive areas of clinical nurse specialist practice. *Clin Nurse Spec.* 2009;23:73–90.

Mastroianni AC. Liability, regulation and policy in surgical innovation: the cutting edge of research and therapy. *Health Matrix.* 2006;16:351–442.

Medically Fragile Children's Act of 2009, H.R. 1117, 111th Cong. § 2(a)(3).

National Council of State Boards of Nursing. Nurse Licensure Compact. 2000. Available at: http://www.ncsbn.org/nlc.htm. Accessed July 16, 2012.

National Federation of Independent Business v. Sebelius, 183 L. Ed. 2d 450 (2012).

National Institutes of Health. Clinical center patients' Bill of Rights. 2010. Available at: http://www.cc.nih.gov/participate/patientinfo/legal/bill_of_rights.shtml. Accessed July 16, 2012.

National Research Center on Psychiatric Advance Directives. What is a psychiatric advance directive (PAD)? 2011. Available at: http://www.nrc-pad.org/content/view/19/25/. Accessed July 16, 2012.

N.C. Gen. Stat. Ann. § 131E-117 (West 2012), Nursing home patients' Bill of Rights. Available at: http://www.ncdhhs.gov/aging/manual/ombud/nhsect2.pdf. Accessed July 16, 2012.

Patient Protection and Affordable Care Act (PPACA), Pub. L. No. 111–148, 124 Stat. 119 (2010).

Pegalis SE. Physician and surgeon liability: standard of care, generally. *American Law of Medical Malpractice*. 2009; § 3.3.

Reinhardt U. Divide et impera: protecting the growth of health care income (costs). *Health Econ*. 2012;21:41–54, 42.

Roe v. Wade, 410 U.S. 113, 93 S. Ct. 705, 35 L. Ed. 2d 147 (1973).

Schloendorff v. Society of New York Hospital, 211 N.Y. 125, 105 N.E. 92 (1914).

Social Security Amendments, Pub. L. No. 89–97, 79 Stat. 286 (1965).

Spencer v. Goodill, 17 A.3d 552 (Del. 2011).

United States Department of Health and Human Services. Fact sheet: the Affordable Care Act's new Patient's Bill of Rights. June 22, 2010. Available at: http://www.healthreform.gov/newsroom/new_patients_bill_of_rights.html. Accessed July 16, 2012.

United States Department of Health and Human Services. A statement by US DHHS Secretary Kathleen Sebelius (news release). January 20, 2012. Available at: http://www.hhs.gov/news/press/2012pres/01/20120120a.html. Accessed July 16, 2012.

Vacco v. Quill, 521 U.S. 793, 117 S. Ct. 2293, 138 L. Ed. 2d 834 (1997).

Washington v. Glucksberg, 521 U.S. 702, 117 S. Ct. 2258, 138 L. Ed. 2d 772 (1997).

Whalen v. Roe, 429 U.S. 589, 607–08, 97 S. Ct. 869, 880–81, 51 L. Ed. 2d 64 (1977).

Wise E. Competence and scope of practice: ethics and professional development. *J Clin Psychol*. 2008;64:626–637.

World Health Organization. WHO definition of palliative care. 2012. Available at: http://www.who.int/cancer/palliative/definition/en/. Accessed July 16, 2012.

Chapter 9

Professionalism and Fiduciary Responsibilities in Health Care Leadership

PHIL B. FONTANAROSA

Effective leadership is critical for the success of any organization, but especially for health care organizations. Leaders have the authority, responsibility, influence, control, and resources to establish, promulgate, and fulfill the organizational mission, vision, and goals (Schyve, 2009). In addition, leaders strategically plan for the provision of services, acquire and allocate resources, and set organizational priorities. Perhaps most important, health care leaders have major responsibilities as co-fiduciaries of patients, as well as for creating and establishing an organizational culture that supports and promotes the fiduciary responsibility of physicians (Chervenak, 2001). Accordingly, health care leaders have a unique and critical responsibility to establish organizational values, priorities, and directions that promote professionalism, and to do so effectively, must demonstrate the highest personal standards of ethics and professionalism.

This chapter will focus on the importance of professionalism and the fiduciary responsibilities of health care leaders.

FIDUCIARY RELATIONSHIPS AND RESPONSIBILITES

A *fiduciary* (derived from the Latin word for "holding in trust") relationship is used to describe a legal or ethical relationship involving trust between two parties. In fiduciary relationships, the parties involved inherently have unequal power, such that one person who usually has less knowledge or expertise, and therefore is in a position of relative vulnerability, places trust, confidence, and reliance in another person to provide assistance, advice, and protection. The patient–physician relationship is a fiduciary relationship, and the fiduciary duty has been recognized as an important standard in contemporary ethics and law.

As described in *Witherell v. Weimer,* "There is no doubt, of course, that the relationship between a doctor and his patient is one in which the patient normally reposes a great deal of trust and confidence in the doctor, accepting his recommendations without question." The relationship is appropriately described in 61 Am.Jur.2d, *Physicians and Surgeons,* section 95, at 214 (1972):

> The relation of physician and patient has its foundation on the theory that the former is learned, skilled, and experienced in those subjects about which the latter ordinarily knows little or nothing, but which are of the most vital importance and interest to him, since upon them may depend the health, or even life, of himself or family; therefore the patient must necessarily place great reliance, faith, and confidence in the professional word, advice, and acts of the physician." (Witherell, 1981)

In this fiduciary relationship, the interests of the trusting person (the patient) must take priority, and the fiduciary (the physician) must always act in the best interest and for the sole benefit of the one placing trust in him or her. According to Chervenak and McCullough, to be a fiduciary of patients requires having "expert knowledge and skills on how to protect and promote the health interests of patients" and being "committed to using that expertise primarily for the benefit of the patient and to making self interest a systematically secondary consideration" (Chervenak, 2003).

This fiduciary duty extends to all aspects of the patient–physician relationship, including the important professional responsibilities of health care leaders as co-fiduciaries of patients. Leaders in health care organizations must accept the requirements of the concept of the responsibility of the physician as the fiduciary for the patient, and establish this overarching principle as the ethical and moral foundation of their leadership and management decisions (Chervenak, 2001). According to Chervenak and McCullough, "Physician-leaders, more than individual physicians in practice, bear the responsibility to shape organizations' cultures that support the fiduciary professionalism of physicians with daily responsibility for patient care, medical education, and clinical research." Moreover, as health care organizations are transitioning to the development of "Accountable Care Organizations," responsible leadership of health care organizations will require "creating and sustaining an organizational culture based on and fully supportive of the full network of co-fiduciary responsibility borne by physicians, organizational leaders, patients, an their surrogates, implemented in preventive ethics policies and procedures" (McCullough, 2012).

FIDUCIARY RESPONSIBILITIES IN HEALTH CARE LEADERSHIP

Some organizations may perceive their fiduciary responsibilities differently than health professionals do. Eiser suggests that in this era of market competitiveness and cost-consciousness, some health care organizations, particularly publicly traded, for-profit companies, may emphasize short-term productivity accomplishments and fiscal outcomes. The professional and ethical principles of autonomy, beneficence, and justice may be overwhelmed by market competition and fiduciary accountability to investors. Rather than emphasizing enhancement of the social good, the for-profit market is more likely to emphasize return on investment, and consider the primary fiduciary responsibility to be to the shareholders (Eiser, 1999).

To fulfill fiduciary responsibilities, leadership of any health care organization engages in strategic and managerial thinking. Schyve points out that this fiduciary responsibility is not the same as financial responsibility, but rather is based on a responsibility that involves trust. Health care leaders must act in the best interests of others, not in self-interest, so that those other constituencies can have trust in the fiduciary. In health care organizations, the fiduciary obligations of health care leaders extend to those who provided the organization with funding, such as stockholders, bondholders, or taxpayers. However, the first fiduciary obligation of health care leaders, regardless of whether in for-profit or not-for profit organizations, is to the patient (Schyve, 2009).

Professionalism requires that health care leaders fulfill those fiduciary responsibilities by assuming responsibility for maintaining the public trust, placing duty above self-interest, and managing resources responsibly. Ultimately, health care leaders have a fiduciary responsibility to ensure that the health care needs of individual patients are met in the context of an equitable, safe, effective, accessible, and compassionate health care system (Fox, 2007).

According to Chervenak, individual leaders in health care organizations must act in accordance with several professional "virtues" and must avoid several "vices" to ensure the moral basis of the professional fiduciary relationship between patients and physicians.

The virtues to live by include self-effacement, self-sacrifice, compassion and integrity; and the vices to avoid include unwarranted bias, the primacy of self-interest, hardheartedness, and corruption. Health care leaders who act accordingly will fulfill their responsibilities to create organizational cultures that support the fiduciary professionalism of physicians (Chervenak, 2001).

Fundamental commitment to the moral nature of medical care is necessary to preserve the medical profession's and the heath care professions' fiduciary responsibility to patients. The development, implementation, and enforcement of a professional code of business conduct in health care will be necessary to ensure appropriate conduct and decision-making for fulfilling this essential responsibility (Eiser, 1999).

PERCEPTIONS OF PROFESSIONALISM IN HEALTH CARE

Health care professionals and leaders are characterized by qualities and conduct that epitomize the profession, such as continuing pursuit of knowledge, responsibility for human concerns, peer accountability, a sense of altruism, and certain degrees of autonomy (DuPree, 2011). Consequently, health care professionals have traditionally been considered among the most respected and admired professionals. In a 2011 Gallup poll in which participants were asked to rate the "honesty and ethical standards" of various occupations, the top three ranked groups (with percent rated "very high/high") were nurses (84%), pharmacists (73%) and medical doctors (70%) (Gallup, 2011). In a 2009 survey in 17 European countries in which participants were asked to rate the "most trusted" professions, the top two were firefighters (92%) and teachers (84%), with medical professionals (including physicians and nurses), tied for third place with postal workers and those serving in the armed forces (all with 81%) (GfK Research, 2009).

However, in light of recent concerns about health care professionals, health care organization leaders, and the health care system, including reports of unethical behavior by some health care professionals, seemingly unreasonable barriers created by health insurance companies coupled with the exorbitant salaries of insurance company executives, as well as vitriolic debate about the ramifications of the Patient Protection and Affordable Care Act (PPACA) and health system reform, public perception of trustworthiness and professionalism among health care leaders may become less positive. Thus, while communities and societies have acknowledged the professional status of physicians and other health care practitioners, and ordinarily have accorded health care professionals the utmost respect, the behavior of health care professionals, especially involving conflicts of interest and undue commercial influence in medicine, does not always reflect these ideals (Dupree, 2011).

In a 2005 survey of 1500 members of the American College of Physician Executives, 90.1% indicated that they were "very" (54.5%) or "moderately" (35.6%) concerned about "unethical business practices affecting U.S. health care," and 33.1% responded that there were physicians within the respondents' own health organization who they believed were involved in unethical business practices (Weber, 2005).

Among potentially unethical business practices, the survey respondents indicated that they were "very concerned/moderately concerned" about the following:

- Physicians' being influenced by pharmaceutical companies to prescribe a certain drug (76%);
- Physicians' being influenced by medical device companies to perform certain procedures (79%);

- Physicians over-treating patients to boost their income (78%);
- Physicians refusing to accept calls from patients who do not have insurance (80%);
- Board members with conflicts of interest (66%);
- Non-physician executive leaders with conflicts of interest (65%);
- Physicians' being paid to make promotional pitches for vendors (61%);
- Physicians accepting gifts from vendors (60%);
- Board members accepting gifts from vendors (58%).

Health care leaders concerned with professionalism and fulfilling their fiduciary duties must be aware of and concerned about the influence of commercial influences and imperatives, and the ability of these forces to erode professionalism. Moreover, health care leaders and executives in all health care organizations and settings must navigate a complex landscape that is influenced by challenging political and social forces, such as shortages of health care professionals, shrinking reimbursements for services and products, extensive requirements to measure performance and report safety indicators, and increasing expectations for transparency, all of which have the potential to affect professionalism adversely (Stefl, 2008).

LEADERSHIP AND PROFESSIONALISM IN HEALTH CARE ORGANIZATIONS

Perhaps as never before, with the dynamic nature of, and changes occurring in, health care delivery and financing, strong professional leadership is needed to reallocate resources, eliminate waste, monitor progress using information technology, engender evidence-based and outcomes-based health care, and envision the future of the health care system (Slavkin, 2012). Effective and principled health care leadership is needed in the academic, private, public, and government sectors; in health care delivery organizations, such as hospitals, academic medical centers, managed care organizations, and accountable care organizations; and in other health-related entities, such as professional societies, health insurance companies, and the pharmaceutical and medical device industry.

Leaders in health care–related organizations may include individuals with a wide range of expertise, training, and experience, and an even wider range of scientific, clinical, business, and ethical knowledge and skills. Those in leadership roles may include health care professionals from medicine, nursing, pharmacy, dentistry, and the allied health professions; health care executives and business professionals with administrative, financial, or legal expertise; and other constituents with relationships to the health care organization or business, such as trustees or members of boards of directors.

Regardless of the background of the individuals involved, leadership in health care organizations generally includes the governing body, the chief executive officer and other senior managers; and in hospitals and clinical centers, leaders of the physicians (i.e., organized medical staff) and other health care professional staff who provide patient care, as described by Schyve. In health care delivery organizations, cooperation and collaboration among these three leadership groups are essential for effectively fulfilling the organizational leadership function, meeting the leader's fiduciary responsibilities to patients, and enabling the organization to reliably achieve its goals of high quality, safe patient care, financial sustainability, community service, and ethical behavior (Schyve, 2009).

As Fox points out, leaders play a critical role in creating, sustaining, and changing the organizational culture through their own behavior and the programs and activities they support or promote. All health care leaders must foster an environment that is conducive to professional and ethical practices that integrate an overarching professionalism into the overall organizational culture (Fox, 2007). According to a study involving interviews with leaders from 30 health care organizations across the country, health care organizations use three strategies to drive professionalism:

(1) Leaders articulated values and drew a clear link between these values and expected behaviors;
(2) Leaders emphasized aligning organizational systems and structures to support desired behaviors; and
(3) Leaders believed that cultivating strong interpersonal relationships within their organizations was key to disseminating and reinforcing organizational values and behaviors. (Cunningham, 2011)

The goal of professionalism for health care leaders is to foster an environment and culture that embodies the highest professional values. According to Fox, leaders in health care are responsible for creating a workplace culture based on integrity, accountability, fairness, and respect. Health care leaders not only have a responsibility to meet their own professional, ethical, and fiduciary obligations, but also must ensure that the entire organization is supported in adhering to the highest standards for professionalism and ethics (Fox, 2007).

Fox and colleagues developed a primer for ethical leadership that provides suggestions for how leaders can support, foster, and improve ethics quality in health care in the Veterans Health Administration. Although this report focused on ethical environment and culture, similar elements are applicable for creating and fostering professionalism and fulfilling fiduciary duties in the organizational environment. Based on these suggestions for enhancing ethical quality (Fox, 2007), following are several key suggestions for fostering and improving professionalism in health care organizations:

- Appreciating that professionalism and ethics are important;
- Recognizing and discussing professional and ethical issues and concerns;
- Seeking and obtaining consultation about professional and ethical issues when needed;
- Ensuring that professional and ethical issues are addressed and resolved on a systems level;
- Perceiving professionalism and ethics as an integral part of quality;
- Ensuring that the organizational staff has clear understanding of professional and ethical expectations;
- Empowering all employees to behave professionally and ethically;
- Fostering an atmosphere in which organizational decisions are perceived as professionally and ethically based.

Fox also suggests that health care leaders should foster an environment and culture that support professionalism throughout the organization. "Professionalism throughout an organization" means that practices throughout the organization are consistent with widely accepted professional and ethical standards, norms, and expectations for health care leaders and staff. These should be reflected in organizational values, mission statements, codes of conduct, and institutional policies and procedures. The interplay of three key levels of factors—(1) organizational and individual professional/ethical decisions and actions; (2) organizational systems and processes that drive decisions; and (3) the organizational environment and culture related to professionalism and ethics—serves to define the professional and ethical quality of a health care organization (Fox, 2007).

To achieve these goals of professionalism requires effective organizational leadership. According to the Joint Commission's leadership accountabilities task force, several issues should be considered for organizational leadership, including the following:

- The organization identifies its leaders and their shared and unique accountabilities (this requirement recognizes that different organizations might identify different individuals as their leaders, and might assign accountabilities differently among those leaders).
- The leaders are all aligned with the mission and goals related to the quality and safety of care.
- The leaders share the goal of meeting the needs of the population served by the organization.
- The leaders communicate well with each other and share information to enable them all to collaborate in making evidence-based decisions.
- The leaders are provided with the knowledge and skills that enable them to function well as organizational leaders.
- The leaders have a process to manage conflicts between leadership groups in their decision making.
- The leaders demonstrate mutual respect and civility with the goal of building trust among themselves. (Schyve, 2009)

An environment and culture that promote professionalism, according to Fox, also serve to enhance productivity, improve efficiency, and improve employee morale. Failure to maintain a culture and environment with highest professional and ethical standards can seriously jeopardize an organization's reputation, performance, and financial well-being (Fox, 2007).

PROFESSIONAL STANDARDS AND COMPETENCIES FOR HEALTH CARE LEADERS

Professionalism, according to Fox, is a core element of health care leadership, and includes ethical leadership, moral leadership, and values-based leadership. Leaders play a critical role in creating, sustaining, and changing all aspects of an organizational culture, including professional and ethical culture. The behavior of leaders affects culture and environment. By promoting and exemplifying professionalism, health care leaders create a climate that promotes and supports professional behavior, and instills a sense of shared accountability among employees for ensuring professionalism (Fox, 2007). When employees perceive that leaders regularly pay attention to professionalism and ethics, take professionalism and ethics seriously, care about professionalism and ethics, and emphasize the fiduciary responsibilities to patients as much as or even more than they do productivity and financial performance for the health care organization, outcomes related to professional and ethical behaviors are more positive.

Specific professional and ethical behaviors of leaders include commitment and proactive effort to model highest levels of professional behavior; development and nurturing of a professional environment; and projecting professionalism, including accountability and responsibility, at all times. Health care leaders should strive to follow their individual professional leadership "compass," which entails: demonstration that professionalism and ethical behavior are a personal priority; communication of clear expectations for professional and ethical practice; always practicing professional and ethical decision-making; and promoting and supporting professionalism and ethical behavior (Fox, 2007).

Standards for Professionalism

The Code of Ethics of the American College of Healthcare Executives includes standards for professional and ethical behavior for health care leaders in their professional relationships. The Code emphasizes professionalism, and states that "healthcare executives have an obligation to act in ways that will merit the trust, confidence, and respect of healthcare professionals and the general public"; also that "healthcare executives should lead lives that embody an exemplary system of values and ethics" (American College of Healthcare Executives [ACHE], 2011).

In addition, the Code notes that

> fulfilling their commitments and obligations to patients or others served, healthcare executives function as moral advocates and models. Since every management decision affects the health and well-being of both individuals and communities, healthcare executives must carefully evaluate the possible outcomes of their decisions. In organizations that deliver healthcare services, they must work to safeguard and foster the rights, interests and prerogatives of patients or others served. (ACHE, 2011)

The Code also states that "The role of moral advocate requires that healthcare executives take actions necessary to promote such rights, interests and prerogatives. Being a model means that decisions and actions will reflect personal integrity and ethical leadership that others will seek to emulate."

The Code provides professional and ethical guidance for the responsibilities of health care executives: to the profession of healthcare management; to patients or others served; to the organization; to employees; and to the community and society as a whole.

- Among the responsibilities to the profession are these: "Conduct professional activities with honesty, integrity, respect, fairness and good faith in a manner that will reflect well upon the profession"; "Avoid the improper exploitation of professional relationships for personal gain"; and "Disclose financial and other conflicts of interest."
- Among the responsibilities to the organization are these: "Lead the organization in the use and improvement of standards of management and sound business practices"; "Be truthful in all forms of professional and organizational communication, and avoid disseminating information that is false, misleading or deceptive"; "Create an organizational environment in which both clinical and management mistakes are minimized and, when they do occur, are disclosed and addressed effectively"; "Implement an organizational code of ethics and monitor compliance"; "Provide ethics resources and mechanisms for staff to address ethical organizational and clinical issues."
- Among the responsibilities to employees are the following: "Creating a work environment that promotes ethical conduct"; "Providing a work environment that encourages a free expression of ethical concerns and provides mechanisms for discussing and addressing such concerns."

Professionalism Competencies

According to the Healthcare Leadership Alliance, *professionalism* is "the ability to align personal and organizational conduct with ethical and professional standards that include a responsibility to the patient and community, a service orientation, and a commitment to lifelong learning and improvement." Within this domain of leadership, there are clusters of competencies, which include personal and professional accountability, professional development and life-long learning, and contributions to the community and profession (Healthcare Leadership Alliance, 2012).

Garman and colleagues highlighted these general competency areas, describing four that are especially important for senior heath care leaders to achieve (Garman, 2006). The first is understanding professional roles and norms, which necessitates understanding formal and informal expectations of conduct, such as by striving to be a model of professionalism within an organization and encouraging professionalism in others.

The second key element involves cultivating and managing working relationships with others, such as effectively delivering and receiving constructive feedback, encouraging others to pursue professional development, and maintaining professional networks with colleagues and within one's professional organization (Garman, 2006).

The third theme of professionalism involves managing personal and individual resources, such as expertise and professional standards, to ensure that roles within and outside of the organization reflect highest ethical and professional standards, and reflect a sense of personal responsibility and accountability for personal and professional activities (Garman, 2006).

The fourth competency for professionalism involves the expectation that the health care leader will contribute to the health management community by serving as a role model, advisor and mentor, and model of professionalism, such as by participating in community service or in service to the profession (Garman, 2006).

Health care organizations are increasingly aware of the importance of their leaders in valuing and promoting professional and ethical conduct. Health care leaders should strive to develop principle-based approaches for ensuring and fostering professionalism in all they do, so that readily apparent values of professionalism will permeate all levels of their actions and interactions, be discussed openly, and become part of everyday decision-making (Fox, 2007). Evaluation and assessment of the performance of health care leaders not only should include quantitative measures of outcomes, such as financial performance, market share acquisition, management of assets, and organizational rankings based on external benchmarks, but perhaps more importantly, should also be based on qualitative measures, such as integrity, character, trustworthiness, communication of mission, and ability to influence (Slavkin, 2012); and above all, exhibit the utmost professionalism

CONCLUSION

Professionalism in medicine and patient care involves much more than interactions and clinical decisions in the office or at the bedside, and also must be practiced and epitomized by health care leaders by upholding the highest values and ethics, practicing principled decision-making, and achieving professional standards and competencies. Physician-leaders in health care organizations must fulfill their responsibilities as co-fiduciaries for patients, and should also epitomize, promote, and protect the fiduciary responsibility inherent in the professionalism of the patient–physician relationship. Healthcare leaders must embody the highest principles of professionalism in fulfilling their leadership roles in health organizations and in ensuring the commitment of the organization to patients' rights and well-being.

References

American College of Healthcare Executives. American College of Healthcare Executives Code of Ethics. 2011. Available at http://www.ache.org/abt_ache/code.cfm.

Chervenak FA, McCullough LB. The moral foundation of medical leadership: the professional virtues of the physician as fiduciary for the patient. *Am J Obstet Gynecol.* 2001;184(8):875–879.

Chervenak FA, McCullough LB. Physicians and hospital managers as cofiduciaries of patients: rhetoric or reality? *J Healthc Manag.* 2003;48(3):172–179.

Cunningham AT, Bernabeo EC, Wolfson DB, Lesser CS. Organisational strategies to cultivate professional values and behaviours. *BMJ Qual Saf.* 2011;20:351–358. doi:10.1136/bmjqs.2010.048942

Dupree E, Anderson R, McEvoy MD, Brodman M. Professionalism. A necessary ingredient in a culture of safety. *Joint Commission Journal on Quality and Patient Safety.* 2011;37(10):447–455.

Eiser AR, Goold SD, Suchman AL. The role of bioethics and business ethics. *J Gen Intern Med.* 1999;14(Supp 1):S58-S62.

Fox E, Crigger BJ, Bottrell M, Bauck P. *Ethical Leadership. Fostering an Ethical Environment and Culture.* National Center for Ethics in Health Care. Available at: http://www.ethics.va.gov/docs/integratedethics/Ethical_Leadership_ Fostering_an_Ethical_Environment_and_Culture_20070808.pdf.

Gallup. *Honesty/Ethics in Professions.* Nov. 28–Dec. 1, 2011. Available at: http://www.gallup.com/poll/1654/honesty-ethics-professions.aspx.

Garman AN, Evans R, Krause MK, Anfossi J. Professionalism. *J Healthc Manag.* 2006;51:(4):219–222.

GfK Custom Research. Firefighters are the most trusted group. June 5, 2009. Available at: http://www.gfk.com/group/press_information/press_releases/ 004151/index.en.html.

Healthcare Leadership Alliance. *The HLA Competency Directory.* Available at: http://www.healthcareleadershipalliance.org/directory.htm.

McCullough LB. An ethical framework for the responsible leadership of accountable care organizations. *Am J Med Qual.* 2012;27(3):189–194.

Schyve PM. Leadership in healthcare organizations: A guide to Joint Commission Leadership Standards. A Governance Institute white paper. Governance Institute. Winter 2009.

Slavkin HC. Leadership for health care in the 21st century. A personal perspective. *J Healthc Leadersh.* 2012;2:35–41.

Stefl ME. Common competencies for all healthcare managers: The Healthcare Leadership Alliance model. *J Healthc Manag.* 2008;53:(6):360–373.

Weber DO. Unethical business practices in U.S. health care alarm physician leaders. *Physician Exec.* March–April 2005: 9–20.

Witherell v. Weimer, 421 NE 2d - 869: Illinois Supreme Court (1981).

Chapter 10

Professionalism, Medicine, and Religion

PATRICIA A. FOSARELLI

... [P]lain people, like doctors and patients, will ask, "What is the right and good thing for me to do? What is *the* good for patients, and what kinds of actions will achieve it?" No one...can escape these questions... [for] there are no patients who are truly nihilists or total skeptics when their own health or welfare is at stake. (Pellegrino and Thomasma, 1993, p. 195).

How does professionalism in religion relate to professionalism in medicine? Although for hundreds of years, the so-called professions have included not only medicine and law, but also ministry, the practical side of religion in more modern times. The Health Insurance Portability and Accountability Act (HIPAA) and the Joint Commission on Accreditation of Healthcare Organizations (JCAHO) include the need for assessment of a patient's religious or spiritual resources and the need for a patient's religious or spiritual care. Hence, a discussion of professionalism in religion is pertinent.

WHAT IS RELIGION? WHAT ARE THE GOALS OF RELIGION?

According to the online *Oxford Dictionary*, *religion* is the "belief in and worship of a superhuman controlling power, especially a personal God or gods." This definition is not completely accurate, as there are some religions (e.g., classic Buddhism) that do not believe in a god at all, personal or impersonal. For that reason, an additional definition from the online *Oxford Dictionary* seems more appropriate: "a particular system of faith and worship." The root of the word *religion* comes from the Latin word *religio* ("obligation," "bond," "reverence") or *religare* ("to bind"). Each religion has its own set of rules that bind its followers to that religious tradition; this binding might be rather rigid or more elastic, especially when a religion allows latitude in terms of individual conscience.

There are thousands of religions in existence, both universal and indigenous. Four religions currently account for 75% of all individuals who claim a religion. In order of number of followers, these four are Christianity, Islam, Hinduism, and Buddhism. Rounding out the top six are Sikhism and Judaism (per "World religions" on the website "Infoplease").

Those believing in divine persons or powers seek to worship them and, to some extent, appease them. Each religion claims to seek "truth," and some claim to possess "absolute truth," which often is at odds with other religions' concepts of absolute truth. This is why there are so many heated debates (and wars) among the adherents of various world religions as to which one is right, since each might have a different view of absolute truth, based on what each considers (divine) revelation and tradition, and the need to defend their concept of truth.

Even in health care, this dynamic can be played out, as a member of one religious tradition attempts to proselytize staff members or patients in order to convert them. Proselytism includes vigorous inducing or recruiting, not presenting one's beliefs to others in a disinterested manner. In a health care setting, such activity is particularly ill-conceived when the one being induced, recruited, or coerced is a vulnerable patient, unable to defend himself or herself from the proselytizer. This is far from the professionalism that religion/ministry ideally embraces.

HOW DO THE MAJOR WORLD RELIGIONS UNDERSTAND THE IMPORTANCE OF CARE FOR OTHERS?

In terms of religion's goals for human beings, although the major world religions differ greatly among each other in terms of beliefs and practices, they all have some variant of the so-called Golden Rule;

> *Buddhism:* "Hurt not others in ways that you yourself would find hurtful." (Udana-Varga 5, 18)
>
> *Christianity:* "Do unto others as you would have others do unto you." (Matthew 7:12)
>
> *Hinduism:* "This is the sum of duty; do naught unto others what you would not have them to do you." (Mahabharata 5, 1517)
>
> *Islam:* "No one of you is a believer until he desires for his brother that which he desires for himself." (Sunnah)
>
> *Judaism:* "What is hateful to you, do not do to your fellow man. This is the entire Law; all the rest is commentary." (Talmud, Shabbat 3id). "Love your neighbor as yourself." (Leviticus 19:18)
>
> *Sikhism:* "Don't create enmity with anyone, as God is within everyone." (Guru Arjan Devji 259)

For these religions, human beings carry a spark of the divine (or the potential to do so) or are the only creatures capable of true enlightenment. That makes the regard for and care of fellow human beings a major tenet of each religion, not an option. Adherents cannot honor the Divine or seek enlightenment in a vacuum; interaction with others is necessary, either because the Divine ordained it or because only human beings are capable of enlightenment. This is the clear message of the major world religions, although some religions have superimposed cultural considerations on religious considerations (e.g., a religion that considers a human being inferior because of the situation of his or her conception or birth). Although the world religions teach respect for all people, some adherents over time and place have intentionally or unintentionally misread the precepts to mean respect for only those who are like them in terms of race, ethnicity, gender, or religious belief. If, however, caring for another person is a proxy for one's regard for the Divine, then such parochialism is unwarranted, since religions that believe in one or more divine beings hold that all human beings were created by divinity to live in harmony with each other.

WHAT DO MAJOR WORLD RELIGIONS HAVE TO SAY ABOUT MEDICAL CARE?

Many centuries ago, and among a number of indigenous peoples even in the modern world, the person practicing medicine and the person praying to the Divine on behalf of the people was the same person. Unlike the post-Enlightenment view of the human being that divides physical from emotional from spiritual, earlier views of the human being understood an interconnection among body, mind, and spirit. The disease a person was likely to incur was related to the person's spiritual state and maybe even caused by it. The converse was also true: the disease could lead to a deadening *or* an enlivening of a person's spiritual state. Hence, the professional practitioner had to be versed in both the medical or healing remedies of the time, as well as the remedies for spiritual distress, because they were all linked. In like manner, the healer had to do what was called for, even if it might place the healer at risk.

Considering the six religions that form the basis of this chapter, it is instructive to note some basic beliefs and how these beliefs influence medical practice. Religions are listed in the well-known categorization as Eastern or Western religions, in order of their antiquity.

EASTERN RELIGIONS

Hinduism

Hinduism is one of the world's oldest religions. Although there are multiple Hindu gods and goddesses, Hindus believe there is only one Ultimate Reality, *Brahman*, which brought into being all that is. Hindus are forbidden to cause harm to *any* living creature by thought, word, or deed. Although all life is sacred, human life is the highest form of life (Fosarelli, 2008, pp. 43–44). Hence, anything that interferes with or destroys life (e.g., abortion, assisted suicide, euthanasia) is forbidden.

Hindus, like Buddhists, believe in *karma*; what a person gives to the world in life—positive or negative—he or she receives back, either in this life or in a subsequent one. Thus, Hindus face illness and suffering stoically, believing that the time of one's death is determined by *karma*. "Hindus believe the body is a vehicle for the soul through which it can experience the world and progress in its journey to God. When the body has served its purpose, it is discarded and the soul takes on another body until it finds union with God" (Metropolitan Chicago Healthcare Council, 2002). For this reason, Hindus do not believe in prolonging life artificially. Hindus believe in reincarnation; that is, the soul is incarnated into many bodies, as opposed to Buddhism, in which there is no enduring soul. However, like Buddhists, Hindus value peace, quiet, and tranquillity when ill and especially when dying (Fosarelli, 2008, pp. 46–47).

Hindus respect medical professionals, and they greatly appreciate when that respect is reciprocated. Professionalism in Hindu medical practice mandates that Hindu practitioners follow certain principles: belief in the sanctity of life, desire to alleviate suffering and provide comfort, respect for a person's faith and autonomy, desire that benefit always outweighs harm, and honesty. Because family is so important in Hinduism, a health professional is expected to include the family in information-sharing and any discussions about care.

Buddhism

In the sixth century BCE, the practice of Buddhism arose from the original Buddha's attempts to make sense of the illness, suffering, aging, and death that he encountered when he first left the protected environment of his palatial home. Buddhism holds that there is a series of rebirths until a person reaches enlightenment, thereby eliminating karma and the need for rebirths. *Karma* is the belief that what a person gives to the world—positive or negative—will return to him or her, either in this life or a subsequent one. Because rebirth is a cause for suffering and death, escaping the rebirth cycle will end both, thus achieving nirvana. A person cannot escape the cycle until he or she becomes mindful, aware that it is the attachment to impermanent things (including life itself) that causes suffering. When a person loses the attachment, he or she becomes free. Hence, the Buddha believed that true relief from illness and suffering comes only with spiritual progress (Fosarelli, 2008, pp. 3–6).

Buddhism has a profound respect for all living things, and so no harm may be done to any living creature. In terms of medical practice, this means that benefit must always outweigh harm. Professionalism in Buddhist medical care requires compassion for the patient, always respectful of his or her dignity and needs, and permits a suffering person to develop compassion to the best of his or her ability, learning from the suffering and illness what they have to teach the person, especially with regard to *dharma* or truth. "If we can accept the inevitability of suffering and impermanence with equanimity, it is like taking a dose of the finest medicine" (Buddhism, Medicine, and Health, n.d.). Mindfulness is not achieved quickly or amid noise and chaos; peace and quiet are essential, especially as a person is dying.

> In the *Sutra of Buddha's Diagnosis,* the Buddha explained that.... doctors must 1) discover the origin of the illness, 2) achieve a thorough understanding of the illness, 3) prescribe the appropriate medication to cure the illness, and 4) completely cure the illness in a manner that prevents it from recurring....A good doctor should always act with a generous heart when treating patients, considering them as his or her dearest friends (Buddhism, Medicine, and Health, n.d.).

Sikhism

Sikhism arose in the fourteenth century in India. *Sikhs* ("disciples") practice devotion to God at all times, for there is only one God. Sikhs believe in the equality of all men, women, and children, regardless of race and creed, and teach a profound respect for all people. For a Sikh, human beings are to live honest lives in service to others and in constant awareness of the Divine within each person (Singh, 2009, p. 13). Sikhs believe in rebirths, but human life is the highest form of life. Abortion, euthanasia, assisted suicide, and the futile prolongation of life are not permitted. Sikhs know that whoever is born must die; every material body dies. But the soul lives on because it is part of God and seeks union with God. That is the meaning of life (Queensland Health, 2011).

Sikhs wear five symbols of their faith, and each of these is vitally important to a Sikh's identity as a disciple: uncut hair, a wooden comb, a steel bracelet, a small ceremonial sword, and a silk undergarment (Singh, 2009, p. 13). These symbols should never be removed from a Sikh patient unless the person (or a family member, if the patient is not alert) has given permission, or there is an absolute necessity for their removal (Queensland Health, 2011, pp. 8–9). Because Sikhs believe in the equality of all people, they are willing to respect the religious symbols of others.

Sikhs believe in medical care but also pray for God's help when ill. They seek peace and forgiveness when they are ill, especially through the words of their sacred scripture and hymns. Like Hindus, Sikhs respect medical professionals, and they also greatly appreciate when that respect is reciprocated. Professionalism in Sikh medical practice mandates that practitioners believe in the sanctity of life; desire to alleviate suffering and provide comfort; respect a person's faith, its symbols, and autonomy; strive to increase the likelihood of benefit over the likelihood of harm; and practice honesty in all matters (Singh, 2009, p. 8). Because family is important in the Sikh tradition, a medical professional is expected to include the family in information-sharing and any discussions about care (Singh, 2009, p. 5).

WESTERN RELIGIONS

Judaism

The Jewish tradition extends back several thousand years. Jews believe that there is one God and that God revealed himself to them through the patriarchs and prophets, as revealed in their sacred scripture. Jewish law has both oral and written traditions, providing guidelines for the proper conduct of the Jewish people among themselves and as they interface with those outside their community (Fosarelli, 2008, pp. 70–71). According to Psalm 34:15, one must not only turn from evil, *but also* do good. For most "do not" rules, there are also complementary "do" rules: for example, do not steal, *and* give to those in need. Passages in the Biblical books of Leviticus and Exodus highlight the need to honor others and to refrain from hating, physically harming, or verbally abusing or slandering others.

Jewish teaching notes that actions must not only be upright, but be preceded by upright thoughts and words. For the observant Jew, holiness can be found in the day-to-day activities with others; this is especially true of extending justice to others. Raising the profane to the holy is ordained by God (Steinberg, 2003, p. 30).

The Jewish tradition has great respect for physicians, while acknowledging that God is the ultimate Physician. In Jewish thought, the physician who acts in a professional manner must treat the patients who come to him or her, using sound medical judgment in doing so.

> The physician–patient relationship in Judaism is not a voluntary contractual arrangement but a Divine commandment and obligation. The patient is commanded to seek healing from the physician and to prevent illness if possible.
>
> The physician is obligated to heal and is considered to be the messenger of God in the care of patients. The patient is not free to decide autonomously to refuse treatment which is beneficial or save his life.... In Judaism, the value of human life is supreme; therefore to save a life, nearly all biblical laws are waived.... The principle of autonomy ... is modified in Judaism. Judaism asserts that man was created in the image of God and that all people are, therefore, considered special and equal. Thus, Judaism requires that all people must respect and help

one another. Judaism also accepts a degree of patient autonomy in the physician–patient relationship... [for] in Judaism, man is said to have free will and choice.... The principles of beneficence and non-maleficence are clearly defined axioms in Judaism, which prohibit the intentional harming of another person either physically, emotionally, or financially, or by defamation or by an attack on objects owned by others. In addition, Jewish law clearly requires not only the avoidance of harm to others but the active doing of good to others. (Steinberg, 2003, pp. 40–42)

Christianity

Emerging from Judaism about 2000 years ago, Christianity shares Judaism's concern for the poor and downtrodden. Christianity holds that every human being was made in the image and likeness of God. This especially includes those who are ill and dying, as Jesus Christ's healing ministry embraced those who were ill. The early Christians followed Christ's lead, and some of the earliest hospitals were founded by men and women in the religious orders who understood they were to care for the ill, based on Christ's example and also his words in the gospel of Matthew 25: "I was ill and you cared for me.... Whatever you do to the least of these, you do to me." This care is to be provided to friend and stranger, ally and enemy (Fosarelli, 2008, pp. 17–19).

Although Christ never made a one-to-one correlation between a person's illness and any wrong he had done, some Christian leaders throughout the last 2000 years did so. That stance is definitely a minority one currently, as most Christian denominations hold that illness, suffering, and dying are all part of a fallen, broken world (Fosarelli, 2008, p. 19). Yet, many Christians still fear that their illness might be a result of their personal sinfulness.

PATIENT CARE AND PROFESSIONALISM

Because of the numerous denominations and groups within Christianity, there is no blanket statement about what a Christian physician exhibiting professionalism would do in certain situations. For example, some denominations approve of abortion up to a certain point in pregnancy, while other denominations (especially Roman Catholicism and the Orthodox tradition) forbid it unless it is necessary to save the mother's life, a relatively rare occurrence. Yet, certain features would mark the professionalism of a Christian physician: willingness to treat each person, regardless of his or her race, gender, ethnicity, or creed, because of the belief that Christ is in each person; respect for human life, especially those at the extremes of life and those with limited mental capacity; respect for patient autonomy and free will; and diligence in trying to bring more benefit than harm in each medical encounter.

Islam

Islam means "to submit," and the adherents of Islam (Muslims) submit to Allah (the Muslim name for God) in all that they do (Fosarelli, 2008, p. 55). Established about 1400 years ago, Islam is a religion of peace and mercy, but modern-day terrorists have given the impression that Islam is a violent religion in the minds and practices of Muslims.

Muslims believe in one God, who has made himself known through sacred scripture (the Qu'ran) and the prophets; the words and traditions of Muhammad (the Sunnah) are particularly respected. The five pillars (or chief beliefs/practices) of Islam are: declaration of the Muslim faith, five obligatory daily prayers, fasting during the month of Ramadan, a pilgrimage to Mecca at least once in a believer's life, and a 2.5% annual offering from one's income or wealth to be used for the poor (Fosarelli, 2008, pp. 56–57). These pillars point a Muslim away from consideration of himself and toward a consideration of Allah and other human beings, especially those in need.

Every human life is sacred, created by God. Because Muslims believe that the length of a person's life is determined by God, devout family members often appear stoic during a loved one's dying. This belief in God's sovereignty over life also means that no attempts to shorten or futilely prolong life can be attempted (Fosarelli, 2008, pp. 56, 58). As a rule, Muslims do not object to non-Muslim medical therapies as long as they are not at odds with Islam. Since the body is sacred and belongs to God, manipulations of a dead body such as autopsies, embalming, or cremation—all permitted in the Western mind—are forbidden. The professional Muslim physician respects the basic tenets of Islam and treats human beings and human life with the utmost respect. The Muslim physician is also subject to *shariah* (Islamic law) (Yousif, 2003).

Muslims believe that Adam was the first prophet in a long line of prophets, with Muhammad being the last. Since Adam is believed to be the father of the human race, all people are brothers and sisters in the human family, and there is no justification for racial or ethnic prejudice or considering one person or group inferior to another. "The Qu'ran and Sunnah eliminate racial pride and claims of national or ethnic superiority" (Islamic Council of Queensland, 1996, p. 18). All people are equal before God, and contrary to popular belief, Muslims do not consider men to be superior to women. In physician–patient relations, however, Muslims prefer to be cared for by individuals of their own gender (Islamic Council of Queensland, 1996, p. 8).

CARE FOR THE "OTHER"

The six religions discussed all value human life as a gift from God (in the five religions which believe in God or gods) and as a high expression of life (Buddhism). This value of human life mandates that care for the ill by physicians of these religious traditions must be provided readily and in the best manner possible. Since no religion under discussion makes a distinction about the worth of a human life of a believer versus that of a non-believer or enemy, professionalism in all these religions requires that physicians treat those who do not share their beliefs or heritages in the same manner (medically speaking) as they would persons who are closer to their own worldviews.

This should not be construed to mean, however, that all patients, even with identical illnesses, are to be treated the same across the board. When religion is important to a patient, physician professionalism must take this into account. This is done in at least four ways:

(1) Finding out what beliefs and practices are important to a patient, especially beliefs and practices that might impact medical care;

(2) Trying to honor a patient's most important beliefs and practices;

(3) Carefully explaining—in understandable language—why a certain practice cannot be honored (if such is the case because of necessity and not because of inconvenience), engaging a patient and family members in the discussion, with inclusion of a clergyperson of that patient's religion; and

(4) Seeking the best resolution to a situation, always taking into account patient autonomy and free will.

There will be times when a medical consideration might take precedence over a religious practice (e.g., a life-saving blood transfusion for a minor child whose parents do not believe in blood transfusions), but these situations are often the exception rather than the rule. It is important for the physician who wants to demonstrate professionalism for *all* patients to either know something about the various beliefs of his or her patients or to have access to clergy consultants who can offer advice.

Some examples of religious practices impacting or even altering medical care: A Muslim patient prefers a physician of the same gender; that can usually be honored. A Sikh patient asks that his or her sacred undergarment not be removed; this can usually be honored. A Jewish patient wants *kosher* food, or a Muslim patient wants *halal* food; this can usually be arranged. One might argue that these examples are easy to accommodate, but even more difficult ones can be accommodated with more time and understanding.

Other examples come to mind: A patient who deeply believes that God is the author of life refuses life-prolonging therapy; after a discussion to ensure that all interested individuals have a chance to voice their concerns, this can be permitted. Elective abortions do not have to be suggested to women for whom abortion is forbidden in their religions. Individuals who believe that dying should be done in an environment of peace and tranquillity, surrounded by family without extraneous individuals present, can die at home or in hospice; if dying must happen in a hospital, monitors can be turned off, soft music (especially hymns) can be played, or chanting of sacred scripture can surround the dying person, with only family members permitted in the room.

CONCLUSION

Professionalism in religion and ministry has a deep respect for the "other" and (in the religions that believe in God) the "Other." Hence, professionalism in ministry often dovetails or overlaps with professionalism in health care, particularly when the care of persons who are at their most vulnerable is at stake. Although it might seem that religion/ministry and science/medicine are often at odds, when both disciplines work—respectfully and humbly—for the care of persons in health and in illness, they are more often allies than adversaries.

References

Buddhism, Medicine, and Health. Available at www.blia.org/english/publica-tions/booklet. (Excerpt from *Buddhism, Medicine, and Health* by Venerable Master Hsing Yun; n.d.). Accessed July 16, 2012.

Fosarelli P. *Prayers and Rituals at a Time of Illness and Dying: The Practices of Five Major World Religions.* West Conshohocken, PA: Templeton Foundation Press; 2008.

Golden Rule, The. Available at www.teachingvalues.com/goldenrule. Accessed July 26, 2012.

Golden Rule, The. Available at www.thesynthesizer.org/golden.html Accessed August 6, 2012.

Islamic Council of Queensland. *Health Care Providers' Handbook on Muslim Patients.* Queensland, Australia: Islamic Council of Queensland; 1996.

Metropolitan Chicago Healthcare Council and Council for a Parliament of the World's Religions. *Guidelines for Health Care Providers Interacting with Patients of the Hindu Religion and Their Families.* 2002. Available at www.j:/capes/ethics/cultural guidelines/cg-hindu.doc. Accessed July16, 2012.

Pellegrino E, Thomasma D. *The Virtues in Medical Practice.* New York: Oxford University Press; 1993.

Queensland Health. *Health Care Providers' Handbook on Sikh Patients.* Brisbane, Australia: Division of the Chief Health Officer; 2011.

"Religion." Available at www.oxforddictionaries.com/definition/english/reli-gion. Accessed July 26, 2012.

Singh H. *Caring for a Sikh Patient.* London: Sikh Healthcare Chaplaincy Group; 2009.

Steinberg A. *Jewish Medical Ethics.* 2003. Available at www.jewishvirtuallibrary.org/jsource/.../JewishMedicalEthics.pdf. Accessed July 26, 2012.

"World religions (number of followers)." Available at www.infoplease.com. Accessed July 26, 2012.

Yousif A. *Muslim Medicine and Health Care.* Available at www.truthandgrace.com/muslimmedicine.htm 2003. Accessed July 16, 2012.

Chapter 11

Professionalism: The Science of Care and the Art of Medicine

JAMES C. HARRIS

"The clinical picture" is not just a photograph of a man sick in bed; it is an impressionistic painting of the patient surrounded by his home, his work, his relations, his friends, his joys, sorrows, hopes, and fears. A physician who neglects the emotional life of a patient is as "unscientific" as the investigator who neglects to control all the conditions that may affect his experiment. (Francis Peabody, 1927)

The essence of professionalism in the practice of medicine is intensely personal. While the biomedical methods used in the diagnosis of disease are objective and impersonal, meaningful engagement with a patient is personal. That engagement is essential in acquiring the personal narrative of an illness, in explaining diagnostic findings, and in assuring adherence to treatment recommendations (Street et al., 2009; Zolnierek and Dimatteo, 2009). Although such engagement is frequently referred to as "the art of medicine," it, too, has an underlying scientific basis. Meaningful social engagement benefits both patient and clinician and facilitates recovery from illness; it is an essential element in a restorative medicine (Harris, 2009) that focuses not only on diagnosis and treatment of disease but also on the reduction of personal and environmental factors that sustain illness. The health professional should take into account the biology of interpersonal engagement and how it influences the autonomic, endocrine, and immune systems in the recovery process. In this chapter, I will illustrate how the art of medicine is a science of care and describe the role of the health professional in restorative medicine.

PSYCHOBIOLOGICAL FRAMEWORK FOR PATIENT-CENTERED CARE

Osler said the physician begins with the patient, continues with the patient, and ends with the patient (Silverman et al., 2008). For him and those he inspired, the patient as a person is central to professional care. Peabody fully captured the physician's role when he wrote that the clinical picture is not simply a photograph of an ill person; rather it is an impressionist painting of someone who is both anxious and hopeful; aware of their past life, individual circumstances, and medical history, but uncertain about what their future might hold in light of the current illness (Peabody, 1927). Adolf Meyer, who introduced the term psychobiology, reminded us that each person is psychobiologically whole, that is a uniquely integrated individual (Meyer, 1915). George Engel's biopsychosocial model (Engel, 1977) revived Peabody's impressionism and harked back to Meyer's psychobiology to provide a framework for comprehensive patient care. The central focus is on the experiencing person, that is not on disease alone but on a patient's "dis-ease" as well. For all of them, and for us today, the narrative of the patient's life and illness is the starting point of the professional clinical evaluation.

BECOMING A PATIENT

Visiting the clinician is a decision, often a reluctant one. Feeling sick involves both experiencing physical symptoms and the psychological interpretation of them (Benedetti, 2011a). Brain mechanisms of motivation and of reward are activated when seeking relief from such discomfort and dis-ease. Feeling sick, a person makes an appointment, anticipating an empathetic medical encounter. Upon arriving in the office, the patient seeks care, and optimally the clinician responds with empathy and compassion. Thus the therapeutic encounter triggers hopeful expectations of help. The science of care pinpoints the neurobiology linked to the steps involved in becoming a patient: seeking relief, encountering the clinician, receiving treatment, and recovering from illness (Benedetti, 2011a).

THE PSYCHOLOGY AND PHYSIOLOGY OF SOCIAL ENGAGEMENT

Meaningful engagement with a clinician should engender trust and alleviate unrealistic anxiety. The clinician–patient relationship has an underlying biology that, when understood, clarifies how a professional relationship with a patient is both a psychological and physiological encounter. I will review the physiology of social engagement before reviewing the psychological aspects.

The human autonomic nervous system has evolved to establish well-defined, hierarchically organized, and discrete emotional states that allow us to gauge our sense of safety in social situations and to trust. Each of these states has its own metabolic profile. These emotional states allow us to respond appropriately to environmental risks and differentially regulate our adaptation to dangerous, demoralizing, and life-threatening situations (Porges, 2001). They are essential to the restoration of physiological homeostasis. These emotional states are: *trust* (meaningful social engagement), *caution* (increased arousal and enhanced vigilance), *demoralization* (declining arousal and self-doubt), and *despair* (reduced arousal and physiological shutdown).

These autonomic neural circuits evolved to facilitate adaptation when a person is stressed and to ensure a means of coping with both interpersonal and physical perceived threats of bodily harm (Porges, 2003). Two neuropeptides, oxytocin and vasopressin, are intimately associated with these neural circuits (Carter et al., 2008). These neuropeptides are persistently active throughout the life span. For example, oxytocin, essential to early mother–infant attachment, persists in modulating adult relationships. It facilitates social engagement and trust. Moreover, oxytocin is neuroprotective. It activates dopaminergic reward pathways in response to social cues. Vasopressin alerts us to danger, enhances caution and vigilance.

Men and women may respond to social stress and threat differently (Lischke et al., 2012; Kubzansky et al., 2012). In one study in humans, oxytocin decreased amygdala reactivity to threatening faces in men, but enhanced amygdala reactivity to similar faces in women, suggesting sex-specific differences in oxytocin (OT)-dependent threat processing. In women, oxytocin may thus enhance the detection of threatening stimuli in the environment, potentially by interacting with gonadal steroids, such as progesterone and estrogen. Therefore, as we consider emotional states, it is important to bear in mind that men and woman differ.

TRUST (MEANINGFUL SOCIAL ENGAGEMENT)

When a patient feels secure and trusting in a relationship with his or her clinician, he or she becomes fully engaged in the diagnostic process. The neurobiology of trust (social safety) underlies the clinician–patient encounter. Trust develops when a patient feels safe with an empathetic health professional. A trusting encounter activates the brain's social engagement network (Porges, 2003). In this situation, patient and clinician establish eye contact and listen intently to each other. Concurrently, heart rate is rhythmically synchronized with breathing—increasing during inspiration and decreasing during expiration (Kemp et al., 2012). This synchronization results from activation of the parasympathetic nervous system. Moreover, through the myelinated vagus nerve, the parasympathetic nervous system innervates the social engagement neural network, which, in concert with the release of oxytocin, regulates the facial muscles of emotional expression and the middle-ear muscles that discriminate human voice (Porges, 2001). These physiological changes underlie the face-to-face engagement of clinician and patient.

Neuroimaging studies provide further information on the anatomy of the social engagement system. One study investigated the neural basis of the perception of faces as "trustworthy" or "untrustworthy." The right-superior temporal sulcus showed enhanced signal change during explicit trustworthiness judgments. Conversely, increased activity in bilateral amygdala and right insula occurred in response to faces judged as untrustworthy (Winston et al., 2002).

Ongoing empathic engagement with a patient may have long-term benefits for illness outcomes in the treatment of chronic disease. One study involved 242 physicians and 20,000 patients with chronic diabetes to determine the relationship of empathetic-treatment-style physicians to outcomes. Physicians completed the Jefferson Scale of Empathy. The patients whose physicians scored high on the empathy scale had fewer long-term disease complications on follow-up (Canale et al., 2012).

Finally, empathetic treatment may boost immune functioning. Besides the heart and lungs, the thymus, densely populated with oxytocin receptors, is part of the social engagement network (Porges, 2001). Thus, positive social contact may facilitate immune functioning.

CAUTION AND ANXIETY (INCREASED AUTONOMIC AROUSAL AND VIGILANCE)

When a patient feels unsure in the relationship with the clinician, he or she may begin to worry or feel threatened. Anxious and sensing danger, the patient's social contact is diminished. Now cautious and vigilant, his or her direct eye contact with the clinician is lost and his or her peripheral vision increases to survey risk; listening is attenuated. With activation of the stress axis, respiration and heart rate increase as the sympathetic nervous system is enjoined to cope with perceived distress and the metabolic rate increases. The patient is no longer fully engaged with the clinician. Such anxiety must be taken seriously. Anxiety and anger activate the sympathetic nervous systems, which elicit the classic fight or flight hypothalamic stress response. Oxytocin release is curtailed, and cortisol and vasopressin are increased to prepare to cope physiologically.

When a patient is anxious, an encouraging word and acknowledgement that the clinician recognizes his or her concerns is reassuring and begins the process of turning off the stress response. Recognizing the patient's anxiety, the clinician might pause in probing about symptoms and ask what seems to be troubling him or her before continuing. For example, a mother took her son for multiple, seemingly unnecessary, emergency room visits for asthma. In the course of reviewing the details of her child's asthma history, she became unaccountably tense and anxious. Wondering why she sought so much reassurance about her son's illness by repeatedly bringing him to the emergency room, the clinician asked what she was reminded of when her son wheezed. She became suddenly tearful and recounted how she had nursed her father, a coal miner, though his terminal respiratory illness with black lung disease. Whenever her son wheezed, she was reminded of her father's final suffering and was consumed with the idea that her son might die if he was not given immediate emergency treatment. Resolution of her bereavement, along with further education about asthma treatment for her son, allayed her anxiety. After these interventions, her anxiety was no longer triggered by her son's asthma attacks.

DEMORALIZATION

When concerns and anxiety are not allayed, the patient may become demoralized, experiencing a subjective sense of incompetence. Jerome Frank has written extensively about demoralization. In discussing demoralization, he stated that it is essential to acknowledge that "all of us must face problems we cannot solve and endure sources of distress that no amount of effort can alleviate" (Alarcon and Frank, 2012). If we do not find the internal resources to cope, demoralization may ensue.

Illness, especially chronic illness, is frequently demoralizing. When demoralized, we are bewildered, disheartened, and confused. Demoralization is linked to the "giving up—given up" complex (Engel, 1977) that may be the result of failing to deal with severe physical illnesses and acute psychological crises. Subjectively, a person loses his or her self-confidence, is pervasively uncertain, and is doubtful about his future. A demoralized person persistently fails to cope with internal or external stress that his and her family or friends expect to be handled (Frank, 1974).

Engel proposed the "hopelessness gesture" as a sure clinical sign of demoralization and emerging despair. Typically it occurs in two phases: reaching out, and giving up. Thus the hopelessness gesture can be recognized in the midst of an interview or examination when the patient sighs, lifts up his or her arms or hands, and reaches out toward the examiner. The palms facing each other are rotated outward, the thumb and fingers slightly flexed as though seeking to grasp. When this subtle reaching out is ignored, there is a flattening of facial expression, and the patient's arms and hands fall back in resignation if there is no response (Engel, 1977). It is a sign that the patient is giving up, and of a shift into an emotional state that is distinctly different from social engagement. This gesture is a red flag to stop, listen, re-engage, and console. Observations such as these confirm the necessity of continuous mutual engagement with our patients.

When I was in Thailand as a Peace Corps physician, the Thai spoke of this kind of dejection as loss of one's protective spirit (*Kwan*), which had "wandered away," abandoning them. Special ceremonies were held to lure the *Kwan* back to restore inner harmony. Similarly, we must lure an emotionally distressed patient back to emotional equilibrium. Loss of self-confidence in the face of illness can be perplexing to the clinician when it persists despite encouragement that is offered.

Demoralization is one of the most common reasons for referral to a psychiatrist (Frank, 1974). Kissane and his colleagues have developed a demoralization scale that identifies five dimensions that may be used in clinical practice: loss of meaning, dysphoria, disheartenment, helplessness, and sense of failure (Kissane et al., 2004). Clinicians can do much to nurture courage and resolve to help maintain each person's sense of meaning in life, their values, and purpose in the face of the adversity that can be an inevitable result of disease and aspects of its treatment. When a person is severely ill, existential issues arise about the meaning of life as a person struggles to cope with death anxiety, personal loss and change, loss of control, diminished dignity, the sense of aloneness, changes in the quality of relationships, and accepting that some things are unknowable. The challenge is to reestablish equanimity, peace, and fulfillment to sustain the patient's engagement with life, despite periodic hopelessness (Kissane et al., 2012).

Several biological pathways may contribute to socially buffering the sense of helplessness and mitigating the stress response. Among these, considerable evidence points to the regulatory effects of oxy-tocin in facilitating social bonding behaviors that modify the stress response. Indeed, oxytocin is a common regulatory component of the social environment when coping with the stress response, and stress-induced risks for mental and physical health (Smith and Wang, 2012).

DESPAIR

When demoralization persists and self-doubt and anxiety continue to increase, the patient continues in the downward spiral from "giv-ing up" to "have given up"; that is, to despair. Despairing, energy is conserved and a person withdraws, becomes more listless, and physiologically shuts down. Gastrointestinal symptoms and bra-dycardia may follow, with the establishment of the autonomic and metabolic of state of despair. Physiologically, despair involves the phylogenetically primitive parasympathetic unmyelinated vagus nerve fibers that innervate gastrointestinal and other subdiaphrag-matic structures (Porges, 2001).

Despairing or giving up is correlated with the onset of disease and with exacerbation of disease. Loss and bereavement impact immune functioning. Bereavement is associated with neuroendo-crine activation of the stress axis (the cortisol response), altered sleep (electroencephalography changes), immune imbalance (reduced T-lymphocyte proliferation), inflammatory cell mobilization (neutrophils), prothrombotic response (platelet activation and increased von Willebrand factors) and hemodynamic changes (heart rate and blood pressure) early in the course of bereavement (Buckley et al., 2012). Conversely, in a recent study *hopefulness* was correlated with enhanced cellular immunity in breast cancer patients based on T-cell measures (Kim et al., 2011).

Stress has been demonstrated to exacerbate neuronal death following stroke and cardiac arrest. It delays cutaneous wound healing, by way of a mechanism that involves stress-induced increases in corticosterone acting on glucocorticoid receptors. Yet in animal studies, hamsters and mice that form social bonds are protected against stress. They heal cutaneous wounds sooner than socially isolated animals. Physical contact experienced by the socially attached pair releases oxytocin, which in turn suppresses the hypothalamic stress axis and facilitates wound healing (DeVries, 2007).

THE DOWNWARD SPIRAL FROM TRUST TO DEMORALIZATION AND DESPAIR

Engel, in his Vestermark Award lecture, provides a compelling example of the downward spiral from self-confidence into despair (Engel, 1980). Engel contrasts the psychobiologically based "biopsychosocial model" with the biomedically focused "disease model" when describing the onset of ventricular fibrillation in a patient brought to the emergency room for evaluation for a myocardial infarction, or heart attack. In doing so, he notes that clinicians' approach to patients and their presenting problems is influenced by the conceptual models in which their medical knowledge is embedded.

With the onset of chest pain while at work, the patient was uncertain of what was happening, but alarmed because of the similarity of his symptoms to an earlier heart attack. Rationalizing and unsure, he continued to work despite his symptoms, seeking to put his work in order before going to the hospital—denying the potential severity of his symptoms. Now cautious and anxious, physiologically his sympathetic nervous system was activated by the stress of his pain. His employer, noticing his sudden busyness, learned of his medical concerns. She told him his health and his family were the important issues now; reassured him about his work; complimented him on his diligence, his devotion to his work, and his integrity. Her concern restored the physiology of social engagement. Relieved by her concern, he regained his composure and confidently left with her for the hospital, anticipating help. By the time he arrived at the emergency room, his pain symptoms had subsided. Activation of the social engagement system though interpersonal dialogue with his supervisor allowed him to regain his composure.

Despite his being stable on entry to the emergency room, the emergency room staff insisted that a full coronary care work-up be initiated immediately. The patient became increasingly anxious soon after the protocol began when there were multiple unsuccessful and painful attempts at arterial puncture by the house staff. Failing after multiple attempts, the house officers told him they were leaving to get help. Left alone, he began to ruminate on the impact of a heart attack on his life, felt resentment that he was in the hands of beginners, and began to lose confidence in his caregivers. Demoralized, as his anxiety increased, he began to despair. Soon afterward, apparently activating the stress axis, he went into ventricular fibrillation that required resuscitation and cardioversion. His biomedically focused clinicians were self-congratulatory about saving his life but seemingly unaware of his psychological distress. The full illness narrative emerged later when the patient was sensitively interviewed and a full case history was taken. Had the patient remained socially supported, had more time been spent reviewing his history (and recognizing his type A personality responses) before the procedures were begun, the outcome may have differed. Had he been reassured, as the supervisor had done, rather than feeling abandoned and left to ruminate, the arrhythmia may well have been averted (Engel, 1980).

When the clinician attends to such emerging signs of anxiety, hopelessness, fear, and emotional disengagement, the primitive "giving up" response often can be prevented. Among the most important psychosocial protective factors against giving up are confiding relationships with the clinician, family, and friends. Allowing the patient to confide and discuss his concerns as the history is taken allays his anxiety. Confiding relationships have been reported to influence outcomes following myocardial infarction and depressive illnesses (Mookadam and Arthur, 2004).

ATTACHMENT STYLE

Attachment style refers to the quality of interpersonal relationships. Attachment leads to the formation of enduring emotional bonds between people, initially between parents and their infants, but ultimately between siblings, peers, romantic partners, spouses, and others in our social world (Porges, 2003).

Mother–infant attachment establishes the quality of emotional relations between parent and infant. Oxytocin provides its biological underpinnings. In infants, children, and adults, attachment is classified as "secure" or "insecure." In general population studies, approximately 60% of people surveyed identify themselves as "securely attached" (Bakermans-Kranenburg and van IJzendoorn, 2009). Securely attached individuals are confident in their relationship with others, while those who are insecure are anxiously attached, compulsively self-reliant, or fearful in their relationships with others. Adult attachment relationships are designated as secure, anxious–preoccupied, dismissive–avoidant, or fearful–avoidant. Knowledge about the organization and stability of mental working models that underlie such attachment styles and how attachment impacts relationships outcomes and their dynamics is important for clinicians. Clinicians should be aware of attachment style when interviewing their patients and take it into account in treatment planning.

People who are more secure in their attachments are easier to engage, to relate to socially, and may be more easily involved in mutual treatment planning. Individuals with attachment-related anxiety are insecure and worry about others' being responsive to them, and tend to require more reassurance from the clinician. People with attachment-related avoidance are dismissive of relationships with others. They tend to be compulsively self-reliant and find it difficult to open up to others. Individuals with attachment related fearful avoidance tend to be emotionally disorganized, especially when stressed. In patient care, it is very useful to be aware of these characteristic patterns of adult attachment: secure, dismissive, preoccupied, and disorganized-fearful.

Children who are securely attached more easily explore the environment and are self-confident, whereas those who are insecurely attached are prone to separation anxiety (anxiously attached) and find it difficult to sustain peer relationships (Bakermans-Kranenburg and van IJzendoorn, 2007).

A classic example of the impact of attachment on physiology is the case of Monica, an infant born with esophageal atresia, which demonstrates how attachment style affects emotions linked to physiological functioning. Monica was fed through a surgically placed gastric fistula, created shortly after birth, for the first two years of her life. Failing to thrive, she was re-hospitalized at age 15 months. An experiment was conducted in the hospital using a paradigm analogous to Ainsworth's "strange situation attachment" paradigm (Ainsworth et al., 1978), wherein Monica's physiological responses to familiar and unfamiliar caregivers were assessed. Striking differences in her gastric physiology were demonstrated, depending on whether she was approached by a trusted caregiver or by a stranger. Positive affect was expressed when the trusted investigator approached. When the stranger approached, Monica showed sad facies, muscular flaccidity, and withdrawal (the despair response). Gastric juice gushed from her gastrostomy tube when approached by the trusted caregiver. But with the stranger, she became quiet and cautious, withdrew bodily, and her gastric secretions ceased. These experiments were repeated over 50 times from ages 15 to 20 months (Engel, 1956).

A contemporary example of the impact of attachment style on behavior is a parent–infant study that examined 30 first-time new mothers to determine whether differences in attachment style, based on the Adult Attachment Interview (Bakermans-Kranenburg and van IJzendoorn, 2009), were related to brain reward and peripheral oxytocin level in response to infant cues. Mothers viewed their own infants' smiling and crying faces during functional MRI scans. Mothers who were securely attached showed greater activation of brain reward regions, including the ventral striatum and the oxytocin-associated hypothalamus/pituitary region. In a second part of the study, peripheral oxytocin response to infant contact during a play session at seven months of age was also significantly higher in secure mothers, and positively correlated with brain activation in both regions. Insecure/dismissing mothers showed greater insular activation in response to their own infants' sad faces and distress cries, activating brain regions linked to disgust, and did not show the rise in oxytocin during play with their infant at seven months (Strathearn et al., 2009). This study provides evidence that oxytocin release can be correlated with attachment status.

ELICITING THE PATIENT'S NARRATIVE

The sensitive clinical interviewer's objective is to establish trust, recognize the patient's emotional state, and consider his attachment status, all prerequisites to elicit the patient's perspective on his illness. The overall goal is to understand the meaning of the illness to the patient and to establish realistic hope about prognosis and treatment. The clinical interview necessarily focuses on the patient's attitudes, fears, and hopes, and not on the diagnosis of disease alone. From this interview and laboratory testing, the case formulation is established.

How the clinical interview is conducted matters. An open-ended or, more commonly, a semi-structured narrative interview includes a statement of concern in addition to eliciting and recording a chief complaint at the beginning of the interview. The narrative interviewer engages the patient by asking about his or her personal life-situation and the context in which the illness occurs. The interviewer allows time for the patient to become personally engaged with the interviewer, who facilitates rapport, elicits facts, attitudes, and feelings, and clarifies the meaning of the illness to the patient. Conversely, the fact-focused structured interview, one the electronic medical record generally requires, emphasizes rational thought and is primarily focused on gathering factual information. The two approaches to interviewing are based on there being two kinds of thinking (logical, or paradigmatic and narrative) that are distinct (Bruner, 1985). One focuses on logical reasoning; its goal is to establish facts. The other produces stories whose goal is plausibility; that is, it seeks to make sense of things—of individual experiences. An effective clinical encounter should include both kinds of thinking, narrative to elicit attitudes, feelings (fears and hopes), and analytic for facts and to clarify personal implications of the illness. Peabody pointed out over eight decades ago that the scientific clinician does not neglect the emotional life of the patient (Peabody, 1927).

Ultimately, acquiring the patient's narrative allows clinicians to be more effective in their care by attending to, reflecting with, and engaging patients as they recount the story of their illness (Charon, 2001). The narrative is told in words, gestures, and strategic silences. The listening clinician follows the narrative thread of the person's story, empathizes as the illness story is told, and enters into narrative discourse with the patient.

Diagnostic listening determines the meaning of the symptoms to the patient who asks: "What is wrong with me?" "Why did this happen to me?" and "What will become of me?" (Charon, 2001). Moreover, diagnostic listening acknowledges that there may be no clear-cut answers to patients' questions. It requires emotional courage for the clinician to bear witness to another person's life's unfairness, losses, and personal tragedies. A narrative interview may allay his or her demoralization by conveying empathy, allowing the clinician to enter into a therapeutic alliance when generating a differential diagnosis, interpreting physical findings and laboratory reports, and arriving at a case formulation that leads to the treatment plan.

If the clinician minimizes the narrative encounter (how the patient seeks to make sense of what is wrong with himself or herself) and focuses primarily on facts, the patient may fail to tell the full story, might be reluctant to ask the most frightening (for him or her) biomedical questions, not feel heard, and leave the office without realistic hope. Without the whole story's being told, the diagnostic work-up may not be appropriately focused and thus be more costly than necessary. The correct diagnosis might not be reached. Clinical care might be affected if the patient feels insecure and uncertain. This may result in the patient's failure to adhere to treatment recommendations and lead him or her to medical shopping in a search for second opinions. Unengaged, the clinician–patient relationship risks being superficial and ineffective. Unsatisfied patients are more likely to follow legal avenues if there are illness complications (Levinson, 1997).

THE PLACEBO RESPONSE

The experience of social trust is linked to the placebo response. (Benedetti, 2011b) Beliefs and expectations may modulate neuro-physiological and neurochemical activity in brain regions involved in perception, movement, pain, and various aspects of emotion processing (Beauregard, 2007). Placebo responses have been linked to dopaminergic reward systems in the brain, immune functioning, and possibly the neuroregulatory release of oxytocin (Enck et al., 2008; Enck and Klosterhalfen, 2009).

Two psychological mechanisms are believed to be linked to this biology and underlie the placebo response: these are expectancy and conditioning (Brody and Miller, 2011). Positive expectations about future outcomes in the context of trusting relationship with a physician may result in better outcomes. Medical routines and rituals may result in conditioned response patterns that may reduce anxiety, and these can be capitalized on in practice. For example, careful instruction about exactly how to take medication at prescribed times may be tied to expectations of effectiveness of the drug treatment and allow a sense of being in more in control of one's treatment—a therapeutic ritual. Offering a clear and satisfying explanation of a patient's illness may remind him or her of the positive social contact during the office visit. Placebo use need not be deceptive, but rather should be aligned with hopeful expectations.

Research on placebos suggests the time has arrived to translate the science of placebo effectiveness and agreed-upon techniques for enhancing and promoting placebo responses fully into clinical practice and medical education. Placebo research is an important component in the science of care.

PATIENT-CENTERED TREATMENT

The patient-centered approach is essential for high-quality medical care. There is broad conceptual and empirical literature on personalized medicine that provides methods of measuring the process and outcomes of patient-centered care (Mead and Bower, 2000).

How medical information is collected has particular significance, because currently, great emphasis is being placed on the electronic medical record (EMR). Differences have been documented in the content and organization of information when paper- and computer-based records are compared (Patel et al., 2000). Paper records tend to have a narrative structure, while computer-based records tend to be organized into discrete items or "fields" of information. Concerns are being raised about how this technology affects the relationship with the patient when the clinician continuously turns away from the patient to enter data into a computer. Issues also are being raised about how the design of electronic record systems, with their focus on gathering factual information, shapes clinicians' cognition. Thus, data-collection procedures and entry into the EMR may affect clinicians' information-gathering style and reasoning strategies (Patel et al., 2002). Consequently, the nature of the patient–clinician dialogue is influenced by the structure of the EMR system.

REALISTIC HOPE

Over six decades of empirical research provide evidence that psychosocial risk factors such as lack of social support, stress at work and in family life, low socioeconomic status, depression, anxiety, and hostility contribute to the risk, onset, and persistence of illness. When the clinician views the clinical picture as encompassing direct recognition of each of these factors that have an impact on illness and understands their role as an advocate, comprehensive care is possible.

The clinician should keep in mind that the goal of the clinical interview is not only to diagnose disease but also (through the illness narrative) to appreciate the meaning of this particular illness for the patient. Knowing this allows the clinician to help the patient establish a realistic hope about prognosis and treatment.

How can the sense of hope be sustained and professionalism maintained today in practice settings where economic forces result in constraints that reduce the time to listen to the illness narrative and threaten continuity of care? Such changes in practice remind us that we must be persistent in reaffirming the importance of listening to the story of an illness. Sharpening our skills for narrative listening facilitates and confirms the therapeutic relationship (Rogers, 2007). Moreover, the dialogue with each patient reminds us of the values of our profession and of our humanity as we face sick and dying patients.

CONCLUSION

The evidence base increasingly substantiates the critical importance of personalized patient contacts and the value of the science of care. As more research is conducted that confirms the neurobiological basis of the clinician–patient relationship, this new knowledge will inform patient care, patient outcomes, and reimbursement practices. Peabody proposed that the essential quality of a physician is an interest in humanity (Peabody, 1927). Such interest by clinicians has not waned since Peabody's time. Human interest will continue to sustain clinicians and stimulate them to advocate for new approaches based on the science of care to meet the challenges of personalized patient care in the twenty-first century.

References

Ainsworth MD, Blehar MC, Waters E, Wall S. *Patterns of Attachment.* Hillside, NJ: Erlbaum; 1978.
Alarcon RD, Frank JB. *The Psychotherapy of Hope: The Legacy of Persuasion and Healing.* Baltimore, MD: Johns Hopkins University Press; 2012.
Bakermans-Kranenburg MJ, van IJzendoorn MH. Research review: genetic vulnerability or differential susceptibility in child development: the case of attachment. *J Child Psychol Psychiatry.* 2007;48:1160–1173.
Bakermans-Kranenburg MJ, van IJzendoorn MH. The first 10,000 Adult Attachment Interviews: distributions of adult attachment representations in clinical and non-clinical groups. *Attach Hum Dev.* 2009;11:223–263.
Beauregard M. Mind does really matter: evidence from neuroimaging studies of emotional self-regulation, psychotherapy, and placebo effect. *Prog Neurobiol.* 2007;81(4):218–236.
Benedetti F. *The Patient's Brain: The Neuroscience Behind the Doctor–Patient Relationship.* New York: Oxford University Press; 2011a.
Benedetti F. *Placebo Effects: Understanding the Mechanisms in Health and Disease.* New York: Oxford University Press; 2011b.
Brody H, Miller, FG. Lessons from recent research about the placebo effect— from Art to Science. *JAMA.* 2011;306:2612–2613.
Bruner J. *Actual Minds, Possible Worlds.* Boston MA: Harvard University Press; 1985.
Buckley T, Sunari D, Marshall A, Bartrop R, McKinley S, Tofler G. Physiological correlates of bereavement and the impact of bereavement interventions. *Dialogues Clin Neurosci.* 2012;14:129–139.
Canale SD, Louis DZ, Maio V, et al. The relationship between physician empathy and disease complications: an empirical study of primary care physicians and their diabetic patients in Parma, Italy. *Acad Med.* 2012;87:1243–1249.
Carter CS, Grippo AJ, Pournajafi-Nazarloo H, Ruscio MG, Porges SW. Oxytocin, vasopressin and sociality. *Prog Brain Res.* 2008;170:331–336.
Charon R. The patient–physician relationship. Narrative medicine: a model for empathy, reflection, profession, and trust. *JAMA.* 2001;286:1897–1902.
DeVries AC, Craft TK, Glasper ER, Neigh GN, Alexander JK. 2006 Curt P. Richter Award winner: Social influences on stress responses and health. *Psychoneuroendocrinology.* 2007;32:587–603.

Enck P, Benedetti F, Schedlowski M. New insights into the placebo and nocebo responses. *Neuron.* 2008;59:195–206.

Enck P, Klosterhalfen S. The story of O—is oxytocin the mediator of the placebo response? *Neurogastroenterol Motil.* 2009;21:347–350.

Engel GL, Reichsman F, Segal HL: A study of an infant with a gastric fistula, I: behavior and the rate of total hydrochloric acid secretion. *Psychosom Med.* 1956;18:374–398.

Engel GL. The need for a new medical model: a challenge for biomedicine. *Science.* 1977(a);196:129–136.

Engel GL. The care of the patient: art or science? *Johns Hopkins Med J.* 1977(b); 140:222–232.

Engel GL. The clinical application of the biopsychosocial model. *Am J Psychiatry.* 1980;137:535–544.

Frank J. Psychotherapy: the restoration of morale. *Am J Psychiatry.* 1974;131: 271–274.

Harris JC. Toward a restorative medicine—the science of care. *JAMA.* 2009;301:1710–1712.

Kemp AH, Quintana DS, Kuhnert RL, Griffiths K, Hickie IB, Guastella AJ. Oxytocin increases heart rate variability in humans at rest: implications for social approach-related motivation and capacity for social engagement. *PLoS One.* 2012;7:e44014.

Kim SW, Kim SY, Kim JM, et al. Relationship between a hopeful attitude and cellular immunity in patients with breast cancer. *Gen Hosp Psychiatry.* 2011;33:371–376.

Kissane DW, Wein S, Love A, Lee XQ, Kee PL, Clarke DM. The Demoralization Scale: a report of its development and preliminary validation. *J Palliat Care.* 2004;20:269–276.

Kissane DW. The relief of existential suffering. *Arch Intern Med.* 2012;3:1–5.

Kubzansky LD, Mendes WB, Appleton AA, Block J, Adler GK. A heartfelt response: oxytocin effects on response to social stress in men and women. *Biol Psychol.* 2012;90:1–9.

Levinson W, Roter DL, Mullooly JP, Dull VT, Frankel RM. Physician–patient communication. The relationship with malpractice claims among primary care physicians and surgeons. *JAMA.* 1997;277:553–559.

Lischke A, Gamer M, Berger C, et al. Oxytocin increases amygdala reactivity to threatening scenes in females. *Psychoneuroendocrinology.* 2012;37: 1431–1438.

Mead N, Bower P. Patient-centeredness: a conceptual framework and review of the empirical literature. *Soc Sci Med.* 2000;51(7):1087–1110.

Meyer A. Objective psychology or psychobiology with subordination of medically useless contrast of mental and physical. *JAMA.* 1915;65:861–863.

Mookadam F, Arthur HM. Social support and its relationship to morbidity and mortality after acute myocardial infarction: systematic overview. *Arch Intern Med*. 2004;164:1514–1518.

Patel VL, Kushniruk AW, Yang S, Yale JF. Impact of a computer-based patient record system on data collection, knowledge organization, and reasoning. *J Am Med Inform Assoc*. 2000;7:569–585.

Patel VL, Arocha JF, Kushniruk AW. Patients' and physicians' understanding of health and biomedical concepts: relationship to the design of EMR systems. *J Biomed Inform*. 2002;35:8–16.

Peabody FW. The care of the patient. *JAMA*. 1927;88:877–882.

Peabody FW. The soul of the clinic. *JAMA*. 1928;90:1193–1197.

Porges SW. The polyvagal theory: phylogenetic substrates of a social nervous system. *Int J Psychophysiol*. 2001;42:123–146.

Porges SW. Social engagement and attachment: a phylogenetic perspective. *Ann NY Acad Sci*. 2003;1008:31–47.

Silverman ME, Murry TJ, Bryan CS. *The Quotable Osler*. Philadelphia PA: The American College of Physicians; 2008.

Smith AS, Wang Z. Salubrious effects of oxytocin on social stress-induced deficits. *Horm Behav*. 2012;61:320–330.

Strathearn L, Fonagy P, Amico J, Montague PR. Adult attachment predicts maternal brain and oxytocin response to infant cues. *Neuropsychopharmacology*. 2009;34:2655–2666.

Street RL Jr, Makoul G, Arora NK, Epstein RM. How does communication heal? Pathways linking clinician–patient communication to health outcomes. *Patient Educ Couns*. 2009;74:295–301.

Winston JS, Strange BA, O'Doherty J, Dolan RJ. Automatic and intentional brain responses during evaluation of trustworthiness of faces. *Nat Neurosci*. 2002; 5(3):277–283.

Rogers CR. The necessary and sufficient conditions of therapeutic personality change. *Psychotherapy (Chic)*. 2007;44:240–248.

Zolnierek KB, Dimatteo MR. Physician communication and patient adherence to treatment: a meta-analysis. *Med Care*. 2009;47:826–834.

INDEX